GUPPIES
Fancy Strains and How to Produce Them

By Noboru Iwasaki
Japan's Foremost Guppy Breeder

PHOTO CREDITS
The original Japanese text did not credit each photo, but
rather gave the following general credits. Those
photographs inside the text which have photo credits
under them have been added to the text by TFH.
Thanks are due to:

Aquastaff, Mr. Iino; Ito Aquashop, Mr. Ichika and Mr.
Kajitsuka; Kitazawa Aquashop; Kinoshita Fish Center;
Guppy Shop, Mr. Koike Brother, Mr. Komatsu; The Fish
Shonan, Mr. Sasaki, Mr. Shiota; Suiso En; Nippon
Aquarium; Big Pen, Mr. Hidejima, Mr. Inishima; Inorenji
Aquarium, Mr. Yara; Lio. . . .and to Chikara Ikeda.

Translated by Anne L. Emig

Distributed in the UNITED STATES by T.F.H. Publications, Inc., One T.F.H. Plaza, Neptune City, NJ 07753; in CAN-
ADA to the Pet Trade by H & L Pet Supplies Inc., 27 Kingston Crescent, Kitchener, Ontario N2B 2T6; Rolf C. Hagen
Ltd., 3225 Sartelon Street, Montreal 382 Quebec; in CANADA to the Book Trade by Macmillan of Canada (A Divi-
sion of Canada Publishing Corporation), 164 Commander Boulevard, Agincourt, Ontario M1S 3C7; in ENGLAND by
T.F.H. Publications Limited, Cliveden House/Priors Way/Bray, Maidenhead, Berkshire SL6 2HP, England; in
AUSTRALIA AND THE SOUTH PACIFIC by T.F.H. (Australia) Pty. Ltd., Box 149, Brookvale 2100 N.S.W., Australia;
in NEW ZEALAND by Ross Haines & Son, Ltd., 18 Monmouth Street, Grey Lynn, Auckland 2, New Zealand; in the
PHILIPPINES by Bio-Research, 5 Lippay Street, San Lorenzo Village, Makati Rizal; in SOUTH AFRICA by Multipet
Pty. Ltd., 30 Turners Avenue, Durban 4001. Published by T.F.H. Publications, Inc. Manufactured in the United
States of America by T.F.H. Publications, Inc.

CONTENTS

Japanese guppies are appreciated mostly for their virility and ease of maintenance. Anyone can raise guppies.

INTRODUCTION

Guppies are appealing for a number of reasons, but perhaps the most important are their virility and the ease with which they are maintained. Anyone can raise guppies with regular aquarium equipment as long as he is careful about such fundamental things as water temperature and quality. You can enjoy different varieties in the same aquarium; one can probably say that the best way to enjoy guppies is to have several of your favorite varieties swimming around an aquarium with a nice layout of water plants.

Hardy breeding being a special characteristic of guppies, no special techniques are necessary. As long as you have a healthy, mature female, offspring will be born. Because guppies breed so well, they are also called "million fish." If one guppy bears 30 fry per litter and 15 of those are females which become fertile three months after birth and then bear several litters of their own, the numbers become astronomical. However, in reality these kinds of numbers are impossible because some of the young are eaten or die and there is also a limit to the number of fish you can keep in a given aquarium space.

Additionally, if you do not separate the parents and offspring, but instead leave them in the same aquarium together, the results will be pathetic. When you raise guppies, you cannot avoid selecting and weeding them out. This is the only way to maintain their beauty.

When your guppy fry get to the point of being able to reproduce you may come to want to try to produce guppies more beautiful than the parent you purchased. Moreover, it is human nature to want to create your very own strain of guppy.

The key to successful guppy breeding lies in selective breeding. Regardless of the strain of guppy, if it does not constantly undergo selective breeding, its quality will deteriorate. This means that, even with systematically bred varieties of high reliability, coloration and design do not reappear exactly the same over several generations; instead, fine changes take place in each generation. Each litter has its own orientation, and controlling how that orientation changes is a challenge.

The aim of this book is to present a guidebook to producing beautiful, healthy guppies. Presented is systematically arranged information on varieties and breeding techniques that have been put into practice over the years. A large number of recent color photographs of guppies are also given as an aid to guppy breeders.

The allowance to breed your own strain of guppy is something not afforded by other fishes. I have a dream of making adults enthusiastic about guppies. I would like to see guppy enthusiasts gather to enjoy their common interests and to exchange opinions and information about guppies.

Domestically produced Japanese guppies.

What Kind of Fish are Guppies?

It is probably not necessary to explain to those already raising guppies that these fishes are killifish, like medaka. Webster's Ninth *New Collegiate Dictionary* defines medaka as "a small Japanese freshwater fish (*Oryzias latipes*) usually silvery brown in the wild but from pale yellow to deep red in aquarium strains." So instead of using "killifish" let's use "medaka" since it's easier to pronounce.

In the medaka group there are medaka, like the Japanese type, in which the female lays eggs and the young hatch from the eggs (oviparous). There are also medaka, such as the guppy, the platy, and the swordtail, in which gestation occurs inside the female's ovary before she gives birth (viviparous).

Among the oviparous medaka is the well known *Nothobranchius rachovi*. Generally, oviparous medaka are said to be rather difficult to breed in that they are highly sensitive to water temperature and quality, and prefer water of low acidity.

By contrast, guppies, platies, swordtails and other viviparous medaka are the perfect introduction to tropical fish because they are hardy, not overly sensitive to water temperature and quality, and are easy to breed. Plus, even to people who have never kept tropical fish, the name "guppy" is well known, just like "angelfish" and "neon tetra."

The guppy originated in the Lesser Antilles island group in the northern part of South America. Guppies either were raised for pleasure and then released or they were stocked for the purposes of mosquito control. Now, they occur "naturally" in Central and South America, the Hawaiian Islands, Southeast Asia and most tropical and subtropical regions of the world.

Recently it has been reported in Japan that "wild" guppies are in the rivers and water lines of hot spring regions. It would be difficult to call these guppies wild in the strict sense. They were born in the suitable water temperature and quality conditions of the warm water drainage lines from guppies that had been kept as domesticated fish but were then set free.

Most wild-type guppies have small bodies 1-2" (3–5cm) with body spots and caudal fins that tend to be rounded. Their most prominent characteristics are their spirited swimming and their strong reproductive ability.

The many and varied types of guppies available today have come from Germany and America (mostly by German-Americans). They were studied very seriously by several geneticists and many books and articles have been published dealing with the genetics of the guppy. Japan is a relatively new country to become interested in guppies...how long will it be before Japanese aquarists can catch up with the rest of the world and produce their own world-class varieties? Look at the photos in this book...maybe they've already arrived?

The many types of beautiful guppies seen today were born as a result of generation after generation of continual selective breeding of these wild guppies by German and American enthusiasts.

However, many have lost their healthy vigor as a consequence of repeatedly being used for selective breeding aimed at enhancing caudal fin and body size. If one looks at recent efforts at breeding a strain, the fish certainly are large and have gorgeous tail fins, but many lack energy.

If one is asked "What kind of fish are guppies?" there is only one answer. They are robust, beautiful fish that swim actively and breed well. At least, this is what guppies should be.

Guppy Origins and the History of Raising Them

The name "guppy" comes from the name of Rev. John Lechmere Guppy, a British naturalist who was one of the first persons to introduce the fish. Around 1865 when Rev. Guppy went to the island of Trinidad on a plant gathering expedition, he discovered the fish and introduced live specimens to England.

However, although it is often said that Rev. Guppy was the discoverer of this fish, in reality it was recognized in 1913 that a Spaniard, De Filippi, was the first to uncover it, having given it the name *Lebistes poeciliodes* two years prior to Guppy's discovery.

Also, in 1859 the German ichthyologist Peters gave a specimen of this fish sent from Venezuela the technical name *Poecilia reticulata*. Separate again from that, the fish that Guppy took back to England from Trinidad was named *Girardinus Guppyi* by Günther who was head of the British Museum, while recognizing *Girardinus reticulatus* as a local race of Venezuela.

In this manner, the guppy had three technical names at the same time; however, in 1913 the nomenclature was unified as *Lebistes reticulatus* by Regan.

However, after that the *Lebistes* genus was incorporated into the *Poecilia* genus, along with the *Mollienesia*, the *Limia*, and the *Micropoecilia*. Accordingly, the contemporary technical name has been settled as *Poecilia reticulata*.

When guppies were introduced into Europe in 1861, there were no more than a few wild fish that were raised for experimental purposes.

After that, it is said to have been around the 1920s when guppies came to be raised as pet fish in England, America, Germany, etc.

In Japan, guppies were introduced to the public in the 1930s; but, until around 1950 there were apparently very few average Japanese who were raising guppies. Guppies came to be raised widely in about 1960.

The boom after 1960 was remarkable, as long-time enthusiasts probably will recall. But whether it was because of the peculiar Japanese characteristic of quickly warming up to something and then quickly cooling to it or because of something else, I do not know; but, after that boom came a lengthy period in which guppies, or more appropriately tropical fish in general, lost their popularity. However because raising dogs, cats, and birds as house pets has become increasingly complicated by housing, civil codes, trouble with neighbors, and the like, goldfish and tropical fish are being looked at again. Guppies seem to have gained in popularity along with the renewed interest in tropical fish.

Rather than a frenzied mania, a quiet boom is preferable, with the raising and breeding of guppies settling in as an adult hobby.

Ways of Enjoying Guppies

There are many ways to enjoy guppies. Beginners raise guppies in one tank together with regular fish such as angelfish and neon tetras. In this sort of case, where the guppy is added as one member of a community, the primary considerations are probably that they be strong and beautiful. If they are healthy, guppies will breed even in a mixed tank.

As the time of birth approaches, one should allow the fish to bear its young in a spawning tank. The young guppies should be kept in the spawning tank until they get a bit larger; when they are big enough not to be eaten by other fish, they can be put into the main tank.

Probably anyone who has kept guppies has experience in this procedure. There are many people who find sufficient enjoyment and satisfaction in guppy breeding and continue to do so for years to come; there are also people who find that guppies breed "too" well and are "too" simple to raise and

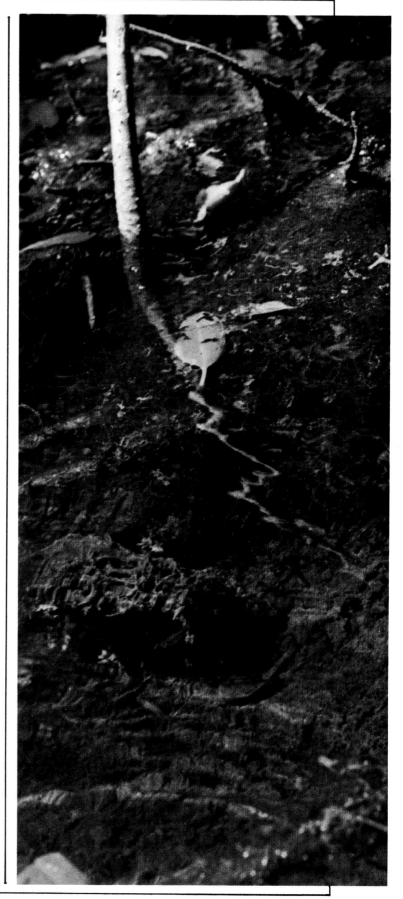

This jungle stream contains lots of guppies. They are practically invisible from the top because of the protective coloration that wild guppies have when viewed from above.

then graduate from raising guppies. This is also fine.

The true challenge and enjoyment of raising guppies lies in creating your own strain of guppy. There is no end to the pleasure found in this kind of experimental endeavor.

The Bottom Sword, the Double Sword, and other domestically bred guppies are almost completely established; thus, you can enjoy them all in the same aquarium. In terms of the breeding technique, you place the parent fish in the aquarium, then, when the female is about ready to give birth, move her into a spawning box to gather the babies. Wait about three weeks; then you can keep the young together with the parent guppies. You should remove any young fish with deformities or poor development as early as possible. In the end you should keep about three pairs that you particularly like, using them as the seed fish for the next generation. By repeating this process, you will be able to maintain a genealogy.

Ordinarily, if you are trying to support one strain of guppy, you need three aquaria. The regular method is to put the seed fish in Tank 1, removing the young at birth. After three weeks, you divide the young into males and females, putting them in Tank 2 and Tank 3 respectively. You continue to raise the males and females separately for at least three months, four months if possible. During this time, carefully watch for fish with poor growth patterns or abnormalities and dispose of them. Then, take two or three each of the male and female guppies and place them in Tank 1, using them as seed fish. If you repeat this process, you can support a guppy lineage.

If you apply this fundamental technique of systematic support for a lineage and increase the number of tanks, you can practice selective breeding to produce new guppy strains.

Guppy enthusiasts can be divided into two categories: the "research group" which concentrates on the enjoyment of producing guppies, and the "appreciation group" whose main interest is in watching guppies and other fish swimming around together in an aquarium. Whichever group you belong to, it is important to master the basics of guppy care and then to establish your own method by adding your own creative ideas, efforts, schemes, and inventions. This is the way to have a long relationship with guppies.

Basic Equipment and Knowledge

Aquarium Size and Selection

When selecting an aquarium for guppies, one must take into consideration such factors as guppy habits, aquarium price, and ease of maintenance. Also, aquarium selection will differ depending on breeding technique and your purpose for keeping guppies.

When appreciation is the principal objective, an aquarium of 15 to 25 gallons is fine. If you have lots of guppies swimming around in an aquarium with sufficient underwater foliage, the aquarium itself can set the mood of a room. If your guppies are healthy, you can look forward to their breeding in the tank.

If selective breeding is your objective in raising guppies, you should make a 20 to 40 gallon tank your main tank. For raising young fish and cross-fertilizing adults, a 10 or 15 gallon tank is easiest to use. In addition, several smaller (3 to 5 gallon) tanks are useful.

For quality and durability, you want to buy brand name products. When you buy bargain equipment and later want to add to your aquarium, problems may arise in obtaining compatible equipment. Consult your pet store owner concerning these matters.

The Filter

The filter functions to clean the water by removing debris (mechanical) and by setting into motion bacteria that decompose the debris (biological),and then recirculating the cleansed water. Also, because it stirs the surface of the water, it stimulates oxygenation.

A variety of filters are available: top filters, undergravel filters, outside box filters, and corner filters that are put right into the tank, etc. Among these, the undergravel filter is especially easy to maintain and its filtration power is strong; moreover, it is inexpensive. Undergravel filters are biological filters and are excellent at breaking down ammonia into harmless nitrates.

It often said that top filters frequently suck up baby fish, but this is something that does not hap-

This is a cannister type pump. It is very powerful and can be used for as large a guppy tank as you will probably ever want. Additional types of pumps are usually available at your local pet supplier. Look through a tropical fish hobbyist magazine to get the nationally advertised brands. The market is full of cheap, undependable air pumps.

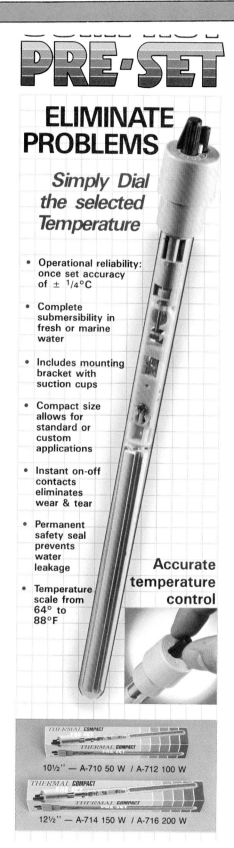

This is an advertisement from an aquarium magazine for a heater which is distributed worldwide. Petshops carry many heaters. Make sure they are nationally advertised and have the features of this one.

pen with guppies. The reason this is not a threat to guppies is unclear. Is this because guppies are not egglayers?

The visual beauty of the tank seems to suffer from an "inside-the-tank" corner filter, but this type is so effective and so easy to use that it cannot be ignored as an option. In raising guppies, where in principle you should completely change the aquarium water once a month, any of the filters are fine if they are easy to use. Which one you choose can be a matter of individual preference.

Light and Illumination

For fish and water plants, light is, like oxygen, indispensable. Water plants, assisted by light, absorb the carbon dioxide in the water and give off oxygen through the process of photosynthesis.

Guppies are active, eat well, and grow in a bright environment. Conversely, in dark surroundings they are not very active, do not eat as well, and experience irregular fertility. Light also exerts a major influence on the coloration and shape of the guppy.

It is best to apply light for approximately 12 hours a day. With less than that, the guppy will not be sufficiently active and the aquarium grasses will grow poorly. By contrast, if too much light is applied, the guppy's rest time will be too short, causing the fish to lose vitality.

When guppies are raised indoors, a fluorescent lamp should be used for light. Many kinds of fluorescent lamps are marketed; but, for plant growth and highlighting the natural colors of guppies, a full spectrum bulb is best. Other lamps for appreciation or for better plant growth emphasize red and blue hues and may mask the true colors of the guppy.

Guppies that are kept outdoors in a garden pond in the summer have a metallic shine to their bodies and their overall coloration is splendid. We do not understand clearly the influence of natural sunlight on color and growth, but I would recommend that you give your guppies some time in natural lighting.

Thermostat and Heater

As for thermostats, the normal bimetal types are rather inexpensive, but there are also electronic models that measure temperature quite accurately.

Heaters come in both submersible and upright

varieties, but I would recommend the submersible because you do not need to worry about breaking it when you change the water. Also, heaters with a built-in thermostat are very helpful. A heater is essential to any tropical tank, but too powerful a heater can cook your fish. Consult your pet store owner for the right thermostat for your set-up.

In keeping guppies, no special equipment is necessary—nothing different from what you use in raising ordinary tropical fish. However, it is important to select the equipment you use on the basis of quality, durability, and convenience of use.

Guppies and Aquarium Plants

It has been said, "With guppies, you should use water sprite " and actually guppies shine in the green of sprites.

Water sprite is one variety of underwater fern. This plant is the ideal partner for the guppy: it likes the same water temperature and quality as guppies; its leaves are wide and soft so they pose no risk of injury to the fish; when they are healthy, they have green leaves that harmonize well with guppies; and they are inexpensive and readily available. As such, this plant is the perfect furnishing for the guppy tank, but there seem to be some people who cannot grow it very well.

Water sprite grows best in water of 22 to 25 degrees centigrade, low acidity (pH 7.2 to 7.4), and a water hardness of relatively 10 to 15 dH. Under these conditions, sprite will for the most part grow well. When the plant spreads, the water becomes clear and transparent.

Other than water sprite, plants appropriate to the guppy tank include *Hygrophila,* water wisteria, and others. Conversely, guppies do not like:

Plants that require root tension (such as the *Echinodorus* genus of Amazon sword and others, or *Vallisneria*) and plants that prefer acidic or soft water such as *Cryptocoryne, Didiplis, Rotala,* and *Alternanthera.* In other words, plants that have weakly attached roots or that are sensitive to changes in water quality are not compatible with guppies because, with guppies, the aquarium water must be changed completely every month.

It takes a bit of work to create a plant layout that encourages the guppies to swim around. If you wish to have a densely planted aquarium, it may be best to use a power filter rather than an under-

The schematic layout shown above and below is suitable for guppy tanks. The side views are the final appearance of your tank. The top views are for your layout.

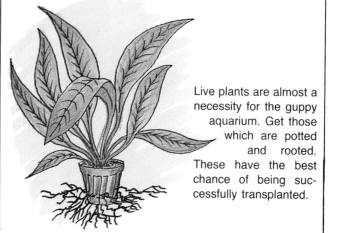

Live plants are almost a necessity for the guppy aquarium. Get those which are potted and rooted. These have the best chance of being successfully transplanted.

You should carefully inspect your guppy aquarium every day. Especially be aware of the water level, pH, temperature and health of the guppies. Drawings by John Quinn.

When changing or adding water, be sure the water is of the same temperature as that in the aquarium. Pour the water in gently so as to leave the plants undisturbed. It is much safer and easier to use one of the many water changers available at your petshop.

gravel one. If you do choose the undergravel filter, you should mix a bit of silica with the bottom gravel to delay the acidification of the water and not plant the plants directly on top of the filter apparatus. To prevent algae, use algae tablets because you cannot use anything with peat in it with guppies. In the case of a planted aquarium, the necessary amount of light increases; so it is best to change the water more frequently. Also, putting the water plants in pots is convenient when it comes time to change the water.

If, however, your purpose for keeping guppies is the pleasure of watching them, you may want to have as many guppies as possible in a tank with just enough aquarium plants to enhance the aquarium setting.

Gravel

In an aquarium without gravel, the water gets dirty quickly, quickly becomes acidic, and does not last a month. If the pH drops below 6.0, the guppy's tail doesn't open well and its caudal fin becomes ragged. If you do not use gravel, you cannot grow aquarium plants, unless you pot them separately.

From the point of view of particle size, components, price, and ease of use, large-grained sand is appropriate to use for gravel in a guppy tank. A layer of sand or gravel about 5 cm (2″) thick is sufficient, keeping in mind maintenance of the plants and filtration.

Preparing and Changing the Water

Success in raising and breeding guppies depends on proper management of the water. If enjoyment is your objective in keeping guppies, then you do not have to take any particular care, but it is a different matter if you are going to carry out selective breeding. In which case, the first wall you'll run up against will be the problem of water.

As for water for raising guppies, if you think in accordance with guppies' qualities and their place of origin, water of 22 to 24°C, pH of 6.8 to 7.2, dH of 10 to 15—water between weak acidity and weak alkalinity. (In reality, a little above or below these numbers is within the range of acceptability.) Guppies are naturally very strong fish, and they are more adaptable than you might think to water of different temperature and quality.

In planning for selective breeding, you ought to know the pH and the hardness of the water in your tank from the start. However, the pH will change depending on the kind of gravel you use and will also fluctuate on the basis of the type of food you use and how often you give it. Here, personal experience with preparing aquarium water becomes important.

It sometimes happens that you buy active guppies with nicely opened tails that have been kept in clear, slightly hard water of proper alkalinity with lots of water sprites, you put them in your own tank and within a week their tails close up; and two or three days later they are dead. This sequence suggests that your water quality is not suitable.

I will explain the basic way to prepare tank water for guppies. With these basics, plus your own experiences, you can prepare suitable water yourself.

First, we use regular tap water, but tap water contains chlorine for disinfectant purposes, so you must neutralize it. Neutralizing agents are available in all pet stores. The amount of chlorine in tap water varies by region and by season, so you must be careful. Often, when we say that "The water there is bad" or "The water in that place smells in summer," this often refers to the chlorine left in the water.

There are many ways of adjusting pH, but usually to make acidic water more alkaline you use sodium bicarbonate and to make alkaline water more acidic you use sodium phosphate. In addition, to preserve low alkalinity in the water, mix quartz/silica with the gravel. Also, you can facilitate water stability by adding some water from another aquarium already in use. Furthermore, by adding a little bit of salt you can increase the hardness of the water and also gain the medicinal benefits of added salinity. The medicines used to treat whitespot disease or tail rot contain a large amount of sodium chloride. However, if you add too much salt, the plants will wither, so it is necessary to use caution.

Once you prepare the water, the next step is changing it. People who cannot change aquarium water cannot raise guppies. Seeing guppies swimming happily in clean water is the greatest joy of being a guppy enthusiast.

The basic principle of changing water is to remove about one quarter of the water once a week from the bottom of the tank and add new water. Then, after one month completely change the wa-

Petshops have a large array of chemical test kits which are invaluable in controlling variables in the water in your guppy tank. Knowing the problem exists is only half the solution. You then have to adjust the pH or DH (hardness) or remove the ammonia or chloramine. That's where a good petshop is indispensable..they should have a wide selection of test kits and remedies.

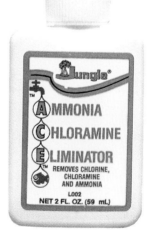

There are literally hundreds, perhaps thousands, of aquarium fishes which can get along with guppies. You really have to depend upon your local petshop to tell you what he has in stock. It's fairly safe to exclude any fish whose mouth is large enough to swallow a guppy whole. You can always remove the guppies if they are in danger. Test the community aquarium fish by putting in some fish which are too old for spawning or showing. See what happens to them.

Special guppy baby traps are available. There are many kinds and many designs. The idea is to isolate the mother-to-be from the other aquarium inhabitants, and to keep the mother from eating her own babies. This is usually accomplished in a floating plastic trap with an inserted, slotted bottom through which the babies fall when born. Drawing by John Quinn.

ter and wash everything beginning with the gravel. However at the time (of the complete water change), you should add in a small amount of the old water. The bacteria reproducing in the old water is good in moderation. Then, it is necessary to take the time to aerate the water, adding the guppies on the following day.

Combining Guppies with Other Fish in an Aquarium

People raising tropical fish for the first time rarely make aquariums of only domestic guppies. Rather, it is common to put guppies in together with various other small fish such as rasboras, neon tetras, or red swordtails. In this sort of mixed aquarium, you cannot appreciate the true beauty of the guppy. Not only that, even though guppies are active, they are rather weak, so if the inclusion with other fish is not carefully considered, it is likely that they will be bullied.

When you have an interest in the beauty of guppies and in selectively breeding them, then you will come to want an aquarium only for guppies. Moreover, as your enthusiasm for guppies advances, your aquaria will increase sharply in number and you will no longer have any interest in other fish.

There are many reasons for raising guppies. If making them part of the interior design is your object, then you would probably gain the most pleasure from an aquarium combining guppies with other docile fish amongst a layout of water plants. In this case, how you display guppies will change depending on what you'd like to emphasize in your aquarium. For example, can you house them in such a way in that the water plants are the main focus and guppies are the detail, or will you house them, as in the usual mixed aquarium, as supporting players with angelfish or neon tetras?

If selective breeding is your purpose, it is best to raise only guppies. Further, it is necessary to be systematic about how you breed each strain.

Guppies have strong breeding ability, so they produce young even in a mixed tank, but if you are not careful in the combination of fish, the other fish in the tank will eat the babies right after they are born. In this case, it is best to allow the female to bear her young in a spawning tank and to raise the fry there until they grow some, then to move them back into the regular aquarium. In addition, you want to be careful of the red swordtail, the barbs, and other fish that have a tendency to gnaw at the large fins of the guppy.

The fish with which guppies can live together are from the *Corydoras* genus which eat the fine threads guppies leave from eating and from among viviparous medaka that are like guppies in their quiet disposition, the black molly and the platy. Also, there is high compatibility between guppies and neon tetras, glowlight tetras and other small characin, small fish of the carp family like red fin sharks, and the rasbora. By contrast, guppies do not do well together with angelfish, discus and other cichlids, and oviparous medaka and African cichlids which have completely different water quality requirements. Guppies of course do not like piranhas, oscars, and other carnivorous fishes; nor do they like fish that snap at their fins such as the tetras.

Cardinal Tetras, shown above, are very beautiful and peaceful enough to live with guppies. Photo by A.v.d.Nieuwenhuizen. Below: *Corydoras trilineatus*, a peaceful scavenger for all guppy tanks. Photo by A. Roth.

The Dwarf Gourami, shown here with the male building his bubblenest, is peaceful enough to be kept with adult guppies. Photo by J. Elias.

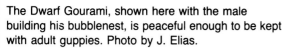

Guppies will eat almost any fish food small enough for them to ingest. There are, however, certain nationally advertised foods which are much better than some of the less scientifically formulated diets available. Ask your petshop for his advice but don't buy any food that isn't nationally advertised in a hobbyist publication.

The problem of topping up or changing the water is made simple by a water changing device which uses the line pressure in your own home to suck water from the tank or add water to the tank.

Feeding

Guppies, being active fish, eat a good deal. For this reason, they will eat as much as you feed them. Because they grow quickly and have a life span of about one year, it is necessary to use food of high and balanced nutritional value.

As for how often to feed guppies, there are some people who worry about the water spoiling, so feed the fishes only once a day. Usually people feed them twice a day, in the morning and evening. Twice a day is sufficient, but, if you can, give the fish some food three times a day: morning, noon, and night. For example, you can feed them tubificids while you view your aquarium in the morning, guppy food around noon, and brine shrimp at night. Zealous enthusiasts may give their guppies a variety of foods as often as ten times a day, but this is not common. This is something that the average working man cannot do. Be careful of foods which claim they do not cloud the water. This is not true. All foods cloud the water if uneaten!

If you always use the same food, the nutritional balance will tilt in one direction or another, so it is best to add tubificids and brine shrimp to the diet along with guppy food. Brine shrimp in particular have high nutritional value and digest well, so they are the superlative food for guppies.

Recently, manufacturers are marketing a variety of foods of good taste and nutritional balance as well as diet supplements; therefore, you can be inventive in combining such products. To give you a concrete example, you can mix a base of guppy food in a mortar together with discus food, conditioning food, and brine shrimp, then crush it and mix it together. Comparing this with ordinary guppy food, it is highly superior in plant protein and vitamins and you can expect it to enhance guppy coloration. Besides this, it would also be good to add beef bone for calcium or to try other creative diet schemes. It is true that the growth, constitution, shape, and coloration of guppies differ on the basis of the kinds of food and how they are given.

For the guppy's body formation, fresh food is important. Guppies like tubificids and brine shrimp quite a lot. Another fresh item that they like to eat well is water fleas (*Daphnia pulex*).

The drawback with tubificids is that sometimes

leeches and various fungi are mixed in with them. Before you feed them to guppies, you should wash them well and use a weak solution of methylene blue; it will have some effect. Put the tubificids in a live-feeder and place them in the tank that way. If you can do it so they do not spill out that would be good. As for brine shrimp, you want to especially emphasize them in the diet of the young fish that need to build their body size. They are also a superior food for grown fish, but if grown fish eat too many of them, they may get diarrhea or develop abnormalities.

The fundamental point about feeding itself is that 2 or 3 times a day will supply the proper nutrition. However, do not give the same kind of food each time; instead, a balanced combination of fresh and prepared foods is best. In addition, because guppies do not eat when it is dark it is best to feed them when the aquarium is illuminated. You will want to be careful of the water quality also because what is not eaten stays in the tank, causing the water to sour.

How to Grow Brine Shrimp

San Francisco Brine Shrimp Company, the world's largest and most reliable supplier of brine shrimp eggs has issued the following information:

Brine shrimp is a feast for both young and full-grown guppies. With its high nutritional value, it is the best food for guppies. Especially for body formation of baby guppies you cannot go wrong with it.

Brine shrimp are in the shellfish group, and what is normally sold is a variety called *Artemia*. The number of days required for incubation differs by place, but among products currently being marketed, a Japanese chemical called "*Artemia* 24" increases the rate of incubation to 20 to 24 hours and it is extremely easy to use.

In order to promote hatching, use an incubation machine, a wide mouth bottle, or a cup. Add an appropriate amount of tap water (the chlorine does not have to be neutralized). Next, add the specified amount of salt. Rather than table salt, you should use the rougher salt (one that is free of additives). If you add an appropriate number of eggs, aerate, and maintain the temperature at about 25 degrees centigrade, the eggs will hatch in 20 to 24 hours. Strain the incubated larva with a cloth and put them in fresh water. Then, gather them in a dropper to feed them to the guppies.

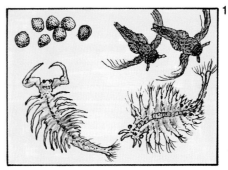

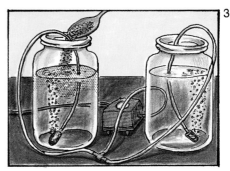
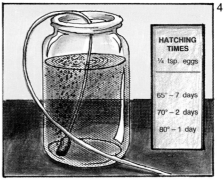

HATCHING TIMES
¼ tsp. eggs

65° – 7 days
70° – 2 days
80° – 1 day

1. Brine shrimp eggs, nauplii and adults.
2. Brine shrimp are hatched in a salt mix which must be aerated. 3. The dry eggs are added to the hatching solution.
4. Read the instructions that come with the eggs as all brine shrimp eggs are not the same.

5. When the eggs hatch, use a strong light to attract the nauplii to one spot. 6. Net them out and then wash them under fresh water. 7. Feed them to your guppies or other fish in the community tank. 8. Using an old aquarium, it is possible to raise the nauplii to maturity. Read the instructions that come with the eggs.

When you give brine shrimp to guppies, ideally you strain the incubated larva in a cloth or a strainer, put them in fresh water, and add them to the tank with a dropper. But when they are busy, people occasionally suck them up from the salt water and put them in the tank without straining them. At such times, salt water is added to the aquarium. Is this a problem?

The consensus seems to be that it does not pose a particular problem, so long as this is done infrequently. This is because only a token amount of salt is used in brine shrimp incubation, and one dropper full of water would amount to only about 10cc of liquid. The smallest aquarium, a three to five gallon tank, contains about 12 liters of water. To add 10cc of a 2% table salt solution to this has virtually no effect. Furthermore, the aquarium water is completely changed once a month, so there is no need to worry. More than worrying about the salt water, you want to be careful not to add unincubated eggs or empty shells to the tank. Aside from inviting deterioration in water quality, they are not pleasant to look at.

Petshops sell more than one kind of water changer. If you are serious about guppies, water changing is a necessity. Having an automatic water changer can make the task easier and less likely to be forgotten.

Illnesses and Their Treatment

Guppies are hardy fish, but they do occasionally become sick as a result of such factors as age, changes in water temperature, and deterioration in water quality. Because they are small fish, once they get sick it is trouble. Rapid detection and rapid treatment are essential.

Most people who have raised tropical fish probably have some experience with whitespot disease. This is a disease caused by parasitism by the whitespot disease protozoan, *Ichthyophthirius*. White spots appear on the caudal fin and body surface. If it is left unattended, these cysts will spread to the whole body surface. By the time the guppy looks like it has had salt shaken all over it, treatment is very difficult, so early detection is critical. If the disease is caught early, it can usually be beaten by adding salt and methylene blue to the water and raising the temperature. In a ten gallon tank, add one small handful of salt, add a few drops of methylene blue so a light color is noticeable, and raise the water temperature 2 to 3 degrees above normal. In addition, a commercially marketed medicine is also effective when used as prescribed. Then, when the guppy recovers, change the water.

If you look closely at this male guppy, you can see small white specks in his dorsal fin. These are parasites called Ich or White Spot. This is one of the early 1950 fancy guppies from Germany. Photo by Dr. Eduard Schmidt-Focke.

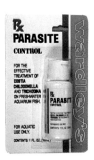

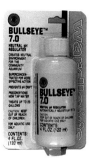

Petshops offer a huge array of drugs and medications to combat almost every aquarium disease to which guppies usually fall ill. Close contact with your petshop is important to every serious guppy breeder. Photo by Ken Levey.

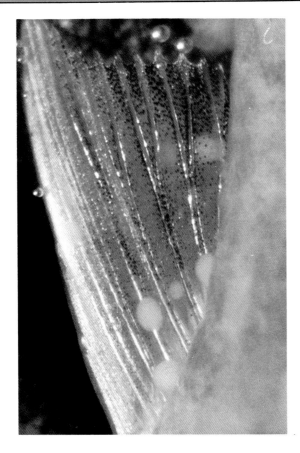

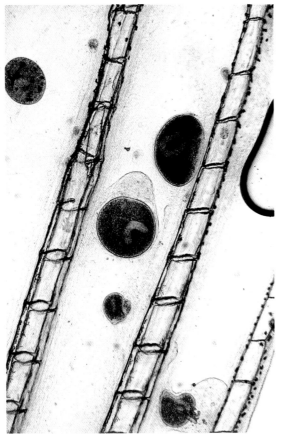

Three photos of the *Ichthyophthirius* parasite. Left: As it looks slightly magnified in the dorsal fin of a guppy. Below, left: Enlarged Ich parasites. Above: The Ich parasite explodes and sends new Ich parasites throughout the aquarium. Photos by Dieter Untergasser.

The most dreaded diseases for guppies are the columnaris diseases of tail rot, gill rot, and mouth fungus. These diseases develop from the parasitic bacteria called *Chondroccus columnaris*. In the case of tail rot, the edge of the caudal fin begins to turn white with decay; with gill rot, the gills turn a dark red color. Eventually, the respiratory system breaks down and the fish dies. Mouth fungus causes the mouth opening to harden, it spreads to the gills and the fish dies within a few hours. In very bad cases, an entire aquarium will be wiped out in one night. Since it is thought that the bacteria grow in dirty water, it is important to check the water every day. If you detect this disease, it is best to move the fish to a tank treated with salt, methylene blue and an antibiotic, and to dispose of any fish that seems even slightly affected.

In addition to these diseases, it is possible for guppies to catch almost any sickness known to tropical fish. After all is said and done, prevention and proper daily care, rather than treatment, are key.

Apart from illness, guppies may also have deformities and/or feeble constitutions. Causes might be environmental deficiencies, diet imbalance, or external injury. Deformities and feebleness from birth may be hereditary, so you should discard affected guppies. Most such cases result from consanguinous mating or other unreasonable breeding efforts.

Imported Guppy Varieties

If you go to a tropical fish shop and look around, you will see many varieties of large, colorful guppies. They may, however, be slightly expensive. These are often imported guppies brought in from Singapore by the tens of thousands of pairs every week.

The process by which Japanese guppy enthusiasts and professional breeders repeatedly sort through these pairs, select out guppies of choice, and carry out systematic breeding is called domestic production. However, the domestically produced guppy does not refer simply to those born in a country by imported guppies purchased from a shop. If we label such offspring F_1, then a minimum of F_2 and F_3 (at least three) generations must be mated before the fish are considered domestic in origin. However, in the exceptional case in which imported blood is introduced for purposes of selective breeding, the F_1 offspring are treated as domestic production.

In comparing the availability of imported and domestic guppies in Japan we find that, excluding specialty shops, tropical fish stores carrying imported guppies overwhelmingly outnumber those stocking domestic guppies.

Until the 1960s, the United States and Germany were the centers for the selective breeding of guppies. Recently they have become consumer countries, being replaced by Singapore as the main production center. At first, the reputation of guppies imported from Singapore was not very favorable: the same variety of female was included in a breeding pair regardless of the male's variety, showing a difference in understanding of the importance of the female in breeding. There were also problems with hybrids that could not reproduce. Such stories were heard during the days of "mania-level" production, when attention was not given to the rate of reliability of the breeding outcome or to whether outstanding offspring would be produced. Most people who purchase guppies do not demand attention to fine points. Instead, they are concerned with whether the guppies are pleasing to the eye and spawn healthy offspring.

These guppies were the winners of the 1970 Singapore Guppy Club Competition. The Singapore breeders were far ahead of the rest of the world in standardizing attractive guppy breeds. The varieties were named, from top to bottom: Double Swordtail Cobra, Tuxedo Flamingo, and King Cobra.

The rare Mosaic Ribbon guppy. Unfortunately, this male is unable to breed because of his malformed gonopodium.

The Golden Yellow Tuxedo is very common nowadays. It is an attractive type.

No matter what, the Neon Tuxedo guppy enjoys tremendous popularity. The neon blue caudal is beautiful.

The Double Sword has very enthusiastic followers. The greenish luster of its coloring is spectacular.

If a wild feeling is what you want, the Bottom Sword is number one. It is well suited to very picky, particular guppy enthusiasts.

A Grass Tail with nicely balanced delicate spots on the yellow caudal fin.

A Red Grass of pre-eminent style. The thick caudal peduncle (connecting area) is necessary to support the large caudal (tail) fin.

The colorful metallic body is characteristic of imported Mosaics.

A Mosaic of strong dark blue coloration. The widely spread caudal fin is a Fan Tail.

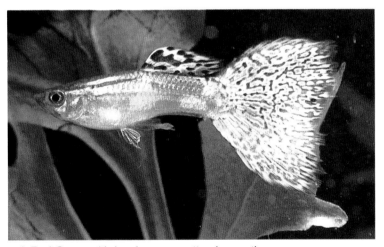

A Red Grass with lovely grass patterning on the caudal fin. This foreign-produced Grass is of high quality.

27

In Singapore, the breeding and exporting of guppies is given favorable taxation and other special treatments due to its importance in foreign exchange acquisition. Industries promoted by government policy tend to be strong, and it is not surprising that they should prosper.

Imported guppies are, for the most part, lacking in the delicate detail preferred by the Japanese, but they have attracted attention for their large size and flashy coloration. Such imports are fine for people interested in keeping guppies only for personal appreciation, offering as they do an abundance of varieties. What's more, Singaporean guppies are so inexpensive that the actual scale and technical sophistication of their breeding industry is surprising, even if you consider the country's lower personnel and fuel costs.

Singaporean guppies are said to be too large in size and lacking in appeal. After Singapore, the guppy industry is most prosperous in the United States, Europe, and Japan, respectively. The large-bodied, flashy-colored guppy is well-liked by Americans.

In Singapore today about 40 strains of guppies are produced; of these, ones with high reliability and a look that suits Japanese tastes number about 20. Incidentally, Red Tail Cobras and Tuxedos are not popular at all in Europe; they are strains geared to the Japanese. In Japan, the red color is very well-liked, capturing the feeling of the rising sun on the Japanese flag. To Europeans the red tail conjures up an image of blood, so they do not like it.

These days, the most popular imported guppies in Japan are the varieties listed below.

Mosaic

The fishes in the mosaic variety are often called Blue Spot, Green Guppy, and the like. With shiny metallic green bodies and large mosaic-patterned caudal fins, the Mosaics are flashy fishes. In females of this variety, the upper portion of the caudal is large and contains a weak flame pattern. These traits seem to appear on all true females.

King Cobra

Usually King Cobras include the Grass Cobra with its grass-like caudal and the Golden Cobra with its golden body and caudal design combining "lace and grass." In this type, the large, individualistic body attracts attention relative to the caudal. Strains are plentiful in the King Cobra family: the

The King Cobra with the metallic green luster. This is a standard coloring for a standard fish.

A robust specimen born from a Mosaic Tuxedo and a King Cobra.

A Red Tail Tuxedo guppy.

The showy yellow golden Cobra is very popular. The lace design in the tail is outstanding.

A King Cobra with a delicate caudal (tail) design. This is a common type guppy in Japan.

This is a popular import from Singapore. It is a Golden Redtail, more affectionately called a Flamingo in America.

Red Cobra, called the Rainbow Jaguar; the Cobra Tuxedo, with its Mosaic Tuxedo tail and its cobra-patterned body; and others.

Grass

In the grass variety are the Red Grass, Glass Grass, Blue Grass, etc. and the Red Glass Grass type which is strongly plated with pink. Sometimes Albino Grass are imported, but the time and the cost of producing them and the problems of supporting the genealogy make the profit base very small, so they are rarely seen these days.

Tuxedo

It is not necessary to go so far as to explain that masterpiece of selective breeding, the Neon Tuxedo. It is a Red Tail Tuxedo with a dark blue body and a tail of transparent red. The Black Tuxedo, popularly called "fox," is completely black below the head. It is plain, but in an aquarium with lots of water plants, it is truly beautiful. The Leopard Tuxedo has black spots on a yellow body. Thought to be related to this fish is the Yellow Tuxedo, with its yellow and black mosaic-design. There is also the strain called Pineapple Guppy that has a yellow tail and a golden body.

Besides these, there are also such strains as the Monochrome Red Tail and the Goldentype Red Tail (which has long been called the Flamingo). Popular Sword strains are the Double Sword with a shiny metallic green body and the Redtype Golden Double Sword.

Also, in the group known as Ribbon Guppies are variant Mosaics and Neon Tuxedos. In order to maintain the genealogy of this type, you mate a bona fide Mosaic or Neon Tuxedo female with a regular mosaic or neon tuxedo type male that has the ribbon gene.

All of the above varieties and strains are highly established and have come to be stable. As a system for a regular supply of beautiful, inexpensive Singaporean guppies becomes more established, quality will get better and better, and a wider variety of strains will be produced.

Problems with Imported Guppies

Despite their magnificence, there are a few problems with imported Singaporean guppies.

First, they are extremely inconsistent. More specifically, there are severe disparities among these fishes in terms of their condition at the time of importation. When they are in good condition, you can put fifty pairs in a tank at the fish shop and only lose two or three before they are all sold. By contrast, when they are in poor condition, the worst case scenario may occur: they are stocked from the place of import, sold and put in a bag and in the few hours it takes to carry them home, more than half the tails will have turned as ragged as a bamboo blind and the specimens will die. The disease is fin rot; it is extremely serious and if the affected fish are put in a tank with healthy guppies, the whole population can disappear overnight. The disease can be transmitted if you so much as put a net used on a contaminated fish into the tank, so it is necessary to be *very* careful.

The cause of the outbreak lies in the fact that so many guppies are imported that to protect them against chafing, a medicinal chemical is applied before shipping them. When they are suddenly moved to water with different conditions, tail rot and mouth fungus set in from the chafings; before you know it all the fish are dead.

Another cause lies in the difference in breeding conditions. Nurseries in Singapore are said to use

A fish farm in Singapore. Photo by Dr. Joerg Vierke.

outdoor concrete-bed ponds which mix sea water in with the fresh water for guppies. Also, if you think about the region, the guppies are being raised at rather high temperatures. When you transfer fish raised in this kind of environment into the home breeding environment, numerous cases will not go well.

As countermeasures, try to avoid the "curse of the first week" after import. Within the first week most of the fish that will get sick become ill and die. Secondly, buy your fish only after carefully examining them; it is best to pass over particularly sluggish fish and those with tremors (the shakes). When you buy fish, do not put them immediately into a community tank; it is best to use a quarantine tank. Gradually remove the salt from the water, and carefully adjust aquarium conditions. Put the newly bought guppies into a tank at about 26 to 28 degrees centigrade with a bit of salt and methylene blue added. Continue monitoring the guppies for a week to ten days, then transfer them to a community tank. If you cannot use a quarantine tank, set the temperature a bit high (27–28°C), keep a close eye, and conditions should be OK.

Doing all this when you purchase your guppies will take time; but once imported guppies adjust to the water they are very hardy and easy to keep.

Next is the problem of males that do not chase females and of the many females with abdominal areas flattened in such a way as to make reproduction seem impossible. These problems turn the catch phrase of guppies, "They are good breeders," on its head.

In any case, you have to look carefully when you choose the fish. Select young fish where the male chases the female, and select the glamorous, full-bodied female. If the female is a little thin, it is best to isolate her from the male, feed well, and then put her back with the male when her physical condition strengthens.

Last is the problem of the female in a pair. Even if the problems experienced until now with imported guppies do not show up and a female reproduces, it often happens that when the baby fish grow up they do not have the same coloration and design of the parent fish or the offspring do not resemble the parent strain at all.

Recently, this point, too, has improved considerably, and for the most part Mosaic and Tuxedo pairs include females of the proper variety. At the same time, you can also say that you get what you pay for with a less expensive imported guppy.

Thus, it is probably best to select imported or domestic guppies on the basis of your own goals and methods of enjoying guppies; if pleasure is your objective, get imported guppies and, if you want to breed guppies, use domestically produced ones.

The basic method of raising domestic guppies has been established to a considerable degree; therefore, the offspring of these fishes will be reliably similar. And thus, anyone can enjoy himself by working on developing a strain. It is also a lot of fun to enter your guppies in contests, to show them to other people, and to hold discussions on techniques of mating and raising guppies.

American King Cobra Lyre Tail or Double Sword Tail guppies from Mac Guppy Hatchery in America (1970's).

These are examples of the Russian Snakeskin or Cobra guppy bred in Moscow environs. Photo by H. Kyselov in 1978. Since that time the strain has been inbred and breeds almost 100% to type.

Winners of the 1970 Singapore Guppy Club competition. Top: Half-blacks or Black Tuxedos. Center: Delta tails with very robust caudal peduncles to help them carry their huge tails. Bottom:Tuxedo Flamingos.

Domestic Guppies

With pets like dogs, cats, and birds, when mating takes place within the same strain, it goes without saying that offspring of the same strain will be born. In mating within the same strain of guppies, it is not necessarily the case that all of the young will be similar.

For instance, when two Grass Tails are mated, there is often a great variation in the color and design of the offspring. In addition to some having caudals in the shape of a Delta Tail, it is rare but sometimes the case that you will find a Sword Tail as well. Moreover, color variations such as Golden or Albino and shape variations like Long Fin sometimes appear.

Only when 100% of the same strain offspring appear is the strain said to be established. If this is the case, then a perfect strain is something that cannot exist with guppies. In reality however, if you produce offspring that to a great extent have the same coloration and tail pattern, it is considered to be a strain. Strictly speaking, it might be more appropriate to call them a "type" rather than a "strain." Additionally, names are sometimes given to a particular hybrid or a unique fish, but in this case it would be more pertinent to call the name a merchandising tool than a type.

Furthermore, even if the rate of reliability improves enough for the term "strain" to be used, use of the correct male and female of the strain in mating remains a major preliminary assumption. Even when breeding from the same litter, if you do not select the true female of the strain, the fry will show considerable disparity.

In this way, strains of guppies are rather unstable. Therefore, it is very important to carry out selective breeding aimed at improving the reliability of a strain and then to maintain it once it becomes "pure."

At present the most stable guppy strains are of the King Cobra variety. This is because the Cobra pattern is normally a dominant characteristic. It is indispensable for selective breeding to know dominant and recessive characteristics and to experiment with heredity.

An important topic from now on in the guppy world will be what we can expect as far as improvement in the stability of strains of guppies.

A History of Selective Breeding

From the latter half of the 1950s through 1960 popularity centered on the Bell Tail guppy. At that time raising and breeding guppies was not a general thing, rather it was the hobby of a limited number of people. The majority of guppies were produced in the United States and Germany, and there was no notion of "domestic" guppies. Later, popular interest shifted to the Fan Tail guppy.

Around 1964 a tropical fish boom began, and this also started a boom in guppies. From 1965 to 1970 was the height of prosperity, the golden age of guppies.

Selective breeding was actively carried out and contests were held in every region of the country (Japan). Every month, magazines printed articles and photographs of guppies and a number of books were also published. It was said that guppy enthusiasts numbered some 30,000. It was also a time of problems, as indicated by some reports about guppies as the object of money-making. Yet, the foundations of selective breeding today were laid at that time.

When King Cobras were first imported by Japan from America, their snake patterning and wild behavior caused a stir. Wild energy and vigorous fertility are the special characteristics of the Cobra variety. Using these traits, many new types were bred: Cobras were mated with Fan Tails to produce the large-tailed King Cobra; the Mosaic Cobra came from the Cobra and the Mosaic; mating the Cobra with the Lace Guppy gave us the Lace Cobra; and the Tuxedo Cobra was a product of mating the Cobra with the Tuxedo.

The Tuxedo variety is of considerable multiplicity and spectacular types have been produced from it: the Red Tail Tuxedo from mating with the Red Fantail; the Golden Red Tail Tuxedo from crossing with the Flamingo; the Mosaic Tuxedo from a combination of the Tuxedo and the Mosaic or the Flame Delta.

Singaporean Fan Tails, a large caudal fin type, were bred with many different varieties. Guppies produced in different countries, unlike today, mixed well with domestic guppies and crossmating was carried out frequently.

In 1969, the German Yellow and the German Leopard were introduced, and in 1971 the Grass Tail was imported. They have taken root as domestically produced guppies. Today, the reason there

The Russian Red King Cobra. Photo by A. Nosnov.

The American lutino (albino with grape eye) Red King Cobra or Snakeskin. Photo by Midge Hill.

The Russian Blue King Cobra. Photo by A. Noznov.

are so many fish that are comparatively easy to breed with the Grass Tail is because it is "new blood."

After this, the guppy boom ended and a "dark age" of tropical fish continued for some time. However, several years ago the enthusiasm for tropical fish reappeared and recently the number of guppy enthusiasts has been increasing. Today, guppy selective breeding is getting started all over again.

This magnificent delta tail was chosen by the Japanese editors to be the cover photo for the Japanese edition of this book. It is a very lovely fish but the ragged tail would be very detrimental in American or European guppy competitions.

Compare these Russian guppies of 1978 quality with the Singapore, American and Japanese guppies of today. It seems that the inbreeding of the Russian guppies made them suitable for further experimentation in western countries. Dr. Herbert R. Axelrod has been bringing back Russian guppies since 1965, breeding them in his fish farm in Florida and distributing the offspring all over the world. The guppies shown above are average guppies sold for 50 kopecks (75 cents US) in the open air market in Moscow. Photo by H. Kyselov.

Classification and Characteristics of Guppy Varieties

The names of guppy varieties come from their underlying color and pattern, and the shape, color, and pattern of their tails. On the basis of color and design we have the Tuxedo and King Cobra, and based on tail shape we have the Sword Tail. Then, in terms of the patterns and hues of the caudal fin we have the Mosaic, Grass, Leopard, Red Tail, etc. Besides these, there are the Albino, Golden, and Tiger whose names come from pigment variations, and the Long Fin which is named for its shape variation.

From here, we can classify Albino, Golden, Long Tail and other varieties that have some rate of regularity and are widely distributed on the basis of the variations within the fundamental genealogy. Furthermore, in cases where there are several characteristics of basic lineages in one type such as a King Cobra with a Mosaic tail, a Tuxedo with a King Cobra design, and a Tuxedo with a Mosaic tail, the guppies are classified by a priority ranking: Tuxedo, King Cobra, Mosaic. In other words, the classification scheme is body color, body design, caudal fin design.

Guppy types that are fundamental genealogies or variations therein, where the lineage is presently being supported, are called strains. They have the characteristics described below. However, like the world's conception of what a beauty queen should look like, the basic standards of a strain change with the times. But those characteristics that are fundamental to a given lineage (such as the dark blue markings on the tail of the Mosaic) must be controlled.

Mosaic

This is a type that has a caudal fin of mosaic-like patterning, as if ornamented with a scheme of inlaid glass or shells. The strains that used to be called Flame Delta and Ripple Tail are also in the Mosaic family.

The body color of the Mosaic is a relatively plain gray, and over that is pale blue or green, with some red, pink, and white also. The color running from

A typical Red Mosaic characterized by a long dorsal.

A Red Mosaic with a flawless large caudal fin.

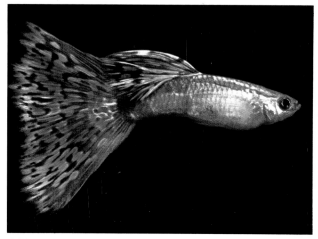
A Mosaic with the same pattern on the caudal fin as the dorsal. It has a perfect Delta tail.

A guppy with a delicately patterned tail. It is attractive because of the metallic blue tint on the body.

A cute Mosaic with a large, wide dorsal fin that looks like a ribbon.

The deep blue hue of the tail is a special character of the Mosaic strain. The large, sturdy body gives the appearance of strength.

Female Mosaics have caudals that widen at the top and have a faint Mosaic pattern.

A large-patterned, two-tone Mosaic of red and black. The widespread tail is spectacular invoking, perhaps, the American cliche: "Peacock Guppy."

the dorsal fin to the root section of the caudal fin becomes a dark blue, although not as dark as that of the Tuxedo. The dorsal fin is a plain white or pale pink but it may have specks. The dorsal is not very large and originally it was quite meager. Mosaics with large dorsals and patterns almost the same as the caudal are thought to reveal the influence of previous mating with Grass.

The most important characteristics are the dark blue caudal peduncle (this is Mosaic's dominant trait and it is the point by which you distinguish it from a Grass) and a Delta caudal fin with a light and dark mosaic design on it. The Mosaic's tail is a very showy yellow where it connects to the body. The body can be a variety of colors like red, green, dark blue, and white. The contrast between the flashy tail that draws your attention and the simple body is quite beautiful. However, the tail is thin,

so when the fish gets older it has a tendency to tear easily.

The Mosaic is a variety that has been around for a long time and is popular with enthusiasts. However, it is difficult to maintain the beautiful tail pattern; the mosaic pattern becomes spotted or runs together.

In the Red Mosaic (a strain with a Mosaic tail of fine red and blue) the upper part of the blue peduncle is white and the part where the tail attaches to the body is yellow, which on a red background appears in assorted colors, among them black, green, and white. This strain has become established and is being maintained. Unfortunately, Mosaic strains outside the red group are rarely seen; it would be interesting to produce a primarily blue or green Mosaic.

On the Golden or the Albino Mosaic strains, the

A Mosaic with spectacular tail coloration which flutters like a flag when the fish is swimming.

A magnificent Blue Mosaic with the characteristic long dorsal and metallic blue body.

A First Prize (Austria) Longfin Guppy, male. Photo by Dr. K. Knaack, 1975.

dark hues of the Mosaic pattern are absent, so it is difficult to create an attractive fish.

The Long Fin Mosaic is seen once in a while, but it is unclear whether the lineage is being maintained. The reason Long Fins are few in number may be that guppy fans tend not to be too interested in them.

Because the Mosaic is a basic variety that is necessary in producing such groups as the Mosaic Cobra or the Mosaic Tuxedo, it is a variety that we want to maintain.

The metallic shine of this Mosaic, plus the interesting pattern of color in the tail, makes this a valuable male.

A variation on the blue strain of Mosaic. This is being inbred hoping to fix it as a permanent strain of Mosaic.

A Mosaic of faint pastel shades. The caudal fin design looks like fireworks.

A blue Mosaic female. She has the same design and coloration on her tail as the male.

This is a well established strain of Blue Mosaics.

These are Singapore champions. Note that the thickness of the caudal peduncle is greater than any fish strain in the world! It carries the large tail proudly. These are Foo Phang Ting's guppies. They were the best in the world in 1972 and formed the basis for all Singapore snakeskins. Photo by Dr. Herbert R. Axelrod.

King Cobra

The name King Cobra was given to these fishes because their bodies resemble the venomous king cobra snake. When these fish were first imported from the United States, the metallic shine of their bodies and the cobra-like designs were so beautiful that they sent a shock wave through the guppy world. Even today, these fishes have numerous variations and their popularity is deeply rooted.

The body color of the Cobra is a characteristic blue or green metallic color. Their defining characteristic is a cobra design that covers the whole body, not dots but a connected pattern. The design is not on the caudal peduncle section.

Sometimes lines alone run sideways the width of the fish (in the case of fish, if the head is considered the top, you look at the fish lengthwise and sideways, so the lengthwise view when it is swim-

ming is really sideways) but this is not desirable. In addition, there are Cobras with red or pink coloration on the peduncle, but the appraisal of such fish is not high. The dorsal fin is not very long; it is even skimpy. As for caudal fin variations, there are Delta Tails, Fan Tails, and Lyre Tails. Caudal patterns may be Mosaic, Grass, Lace, etc.

Because the Cobra pattern is normally a dominant trait, many types can be created through crossbreeding, but the relatively stabilized types are as follows:

KING COBRA. Ordinarily, Cobra indicates a metallic, shiny body with a Delta tail of a yellow and black Mosaic or Grass caudal marking. The dorsal is not very large but through selective breeding it has become longer and bigger than before.

This type is the standard of a King Cobra strain. Males are used to maintain other Cobra lines. Females are mated with males of the Mosaic or Leopard strains to restore body size to females of the latter types.

MOSAIC COBRA. These have metallic bodies of blue, green, and light purple color. Their tails are Delta types of Mosaic patterning. Previously, they were produced by mating King Cobras with Fan Tails, but recent Mosaic Cobras have become established through crossbreeding Mosaic females with King Cobra males and selecting the best, blended specimens in the F_1.

LACE COBRA. The Lace that we talk about here is different from that which was previously called a Lace Guppy. As for the Lace Guppy, the lined pattern on the caudal peduncle piping was called "lace" but the lace of the Lace Cobra refers to a fine design that appears on the dorsal and caudal fins like lace curtains, a design similar to the Lace Tail.

The Cobra of lace design turns up in the F_1 from the crossbreeding of a King Cobra male with a Bottom Sword female. Today, the Lace Cobra that are being supported as a strain have two tail shapes, the Delta Tail and the Lyre Tail. Neither of them is completely established. When a Delta Tail or King Cobra turns up from a Lyre Lace, or conversely a Lyre Lace comes from a Deltatailed Lace Cobra, you cannot classify them.

The elegance of the delicate design makes this a very beautiful strain.

This is a magnificent King Cobra with a delta lacetail. Finding fish this well marked is very difficult.

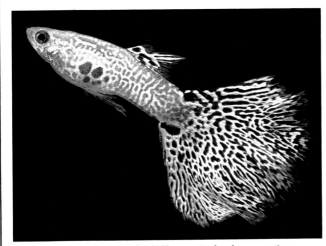

The monocle-like spots look like part of a face on the body markings of this King Cobra.

A marvelous specimen of a King Cobra with its elongated dorsal and magnificent caudal.

A King Cobra guppy with delicately fine patterning.

The Cobra pattern is a dominant feature. The strong markings on this fish, combining tiger, leopard and snakeskin, plus its spread but small dorsal make this fish difficult to classify. The Japanese call it a King Cobra.

The full body and large dorsal fin are wonderful. The King Cobra pattern covers the whole body.

A King Cobra in motion, probably flirting with a female.

The King Cobra female has rounded fins and a pale yellow coloration. In some strains, the female also has some dark spots.

A King Cobra with contrasting yellow and black.

A King Cobra produced by crossing a King Cobra with a Red Mosaic female.

An uncharacteristic Red Tail King Cobra which is quite unnatural for a King Cobra. Several breeders are working on perfecting this strain. The red color in the tail doesn't go with the rest of the body.

A Longfinned King Cobra with a red tail. This is a spectacular fish.

A Lace King Cobra that combines a Lyretail and a Delta tail. The black blotches called "monocles" or "one eyed" in Japanese, are an undesirable trait and prove that the strain is not yet fixed.

A Swordtail Lace Cobra. Thus far this is a wild card and has appeared singularly. Constant inbreeding might fix this lovely strain.

A Longfinned Lace King Cobra. This graceful fish looks like a ballet dancer with silken veils.

A Lyretail, or Double Swordtail as it is sometimes erroneously called, King Cobra.

The Goldentype Cobra has a caudal that easily rips. Compared to regular varieties there are not many fish of this type that are well balanced. Further, if you mate two fish from the same Golden type, many of the offspring are poorly developed or of feeble constitution; thus, supporting the lineage becomes difficult.

The ALBINO COBRA, with many magnificent specimens, enjoys high popularity.

The LONG FIN COBRA has also become a popular variety. Maintaining the genealogy is comparatively easy. However, it is necessary to exercise caution when mating them with other strains because once Long Fin blood gets into a line, it exerts influence on offspring in the distant future. No matter what you say, the Long Fin variety of the Lace Cobra has nobility; it is a superb specimen.

Other than these types, you can also try your hand with the RED TAIL COBRA, the ALBINO RED TAIL COBRA, and the ALBINO KING COBRA of the Long Tail type.

FACING PAGE: The Russian guppy breeders have fixed this strain in 1975. They are able to produce three types of King Cobra. The top fish is the ideal with the red King Cobra pattern in dorsal and caudal fins. The center fish has only long tiger stripes without the red on the dorsal, with little color on the body.The bottom fish has a short dorsai. Note how thick the caudal peduncle is on these fish. Photo by H. Kyselov.

BELOW: This is a unique strain of red King Cobra albinos with dark eyes (lutinos). It is one of many interesting, well-bred strains of King Cobras available in Russia. Photo by H. Kyselov.

An early strain of Cobras, developed in Germany in 1972. These Lyretails, called "Double Swords" in Germany, also feature the objectionable "monocle" spots. Note the female! She seems to be changing into a male. Photographer unknown.

This Grass guppy was the winner of the Japanese Guppy Society's Grand Prize in 1988. The magnificent tail and the very delicate tiny spots with a uniform pattern made it a sensation. Banzai!

BELOW: This magnificent Grass has an amazing tail and a stout caudal peduncle to support it. The tail design is dazzling.

Grass Tail

As far as the recent Grass Tails are concerned, numerous types are produced over and above the Grass Grass and the Glass Grass: Red Grass, Blue Grass, Yellow Grass, and their variations. If we present their contemporary characteristics, we have the following classifications:

GRASS GRASS. The body coloration is a blue or green metallic, with orange over it. The dorsal fin is large and thick. This specimen's special characteristic is its caudal fin. Compared to a Mosaic it is detailed like grass and it spreads widely.

GLASS GRASS. This type is close to the Grass that was first imported. Against a background that is transparent like glass, spot markings in red, blue, yellow, black, etc., appear. The caudal fin of such beautiful, delicate patterning reminds you of stained glass.

RED GRASS. When you crossbreed a Red (Shibame) Grass and a Mosaic, fish with qualities somewhere in between the two appear in F_1. Previously these were called "Grass" and they were treated as "in betweens." But they were established as a single variety after emphasis was placed on selecting and weeding out the best specimens. As long as you select the correct female, 100% of the offspring should turn out to be the same.

BLUE GRASS. The Blue Grass has a body of a metallic blue shade with pale blue spots on it. The widely extended caudal fin has dark blue spots against a blue background. Introduced in a magazine in 1985, it has gathered great popularity to become a leading star of the recent guppy boom.

YELLOW GRASS. The Yellow Grass is a new type produced by crossbreeding with the Leopard, and it is not yet established as a strain. It has a

This Grass Tail of the Glass strain is prized for the round spots in the dorsal and small spots in the tail.

This Grass guppy is a proud looking fish, but the dorsal fin is a bit small for a modern show fish.

This Grass has a wonderful fin spread, a nice long dorsal and swims in a streamlined manner.

This fish looks like a twin of the fish on the upper right facing page, but it is from a different strain even though both are Grass guppies.

Above: This white-tailed Tuxedo from Germany was supposed to throw off Glass-Grass babies when crossed with a Grass. Photo by Dr. Walter Foersch. **Below:** A Red Grass of the so-called "Guramo" strain. It was bred from a Mosaic and a Grass.

A Red Grass of the so-called Glass-Grassblade strain. The neat, well-arranged grass design in the dorsal is beautiful.

The best type of female for the Grass is plainly colored with a rounded tail fin. Some strains have spots in their tails.

spotted caudal against a yellow background, and differences with the Leopard are ambiguous. One would think that if it were specified that black Grass markings appear on the yellow background, then Grass characteristics would be clarified.

Others

The Grasstailed Golden type exists in each respective variety, but the elegant Golden of the Glass variety appears to be the most beautiful. In the case of Grass Tails, unlike the Cobra, if you mate two Goldens, the offspring do not deteriorate in quality.

The Grasstailed Albino presents a fine appearance as the red and yellow colors remain on the caudal; it is quite flashy. I'm not sure if it is because it has new blood or not, but the maintenance of its lineage is better than that of the King Cobra.

This youthful Red Grass is a well established strain in Japan. It is the fancy guppy that beginners are advised to buy.

A lovely Grass which is in the process of evolution in the tail design. It is not prized for this mixed pattern.

BELOW: The large spots in the dorsal of this Red Grass are a simple matter of inbreeding.

The Grasstailed Long Fin is not seen much these days but it is a beautiful, showy fish.

At contests, there are more Grass entries than any other type, and their quality is high. It is relatively easy to preserve its shape, so if you can get your hands on a superior quality seed fish parent, even beginners can enjoy producing them.

LEOPARD. The Leopard is a variety introduced from Germany in 1969. A strain called the American Leopard was also imported from the United States, but its genealogy was not maintained.

This strain was given its name because the leopard pattern on the basically yellow caudal suggested a leopard. The dorsal fin is meager and the body color is pale, but it has a dignified beauty. Lately, you do not see superior fish of this type. I would like to see importance placed on supporting this genealogy.

American Water Sprite plants suit guppies very well. This fish has a nice tail but it seems too large for the fish's body to carry.

A 4 month old Grasstail. It will become more and more beautiful as time goes on.

A female Grasstail, with her large body, is capable of bearing as many as 100 young.

A very nice fish but the yellow hues in the caudal need considerable strengthening. The caudal peduncle is also a bit weak.

This Grass has a lovely tail but its dorsal fin is too small.

A modern Leopard Grass of the highest quality. The tail fin of this young fish will probably grow longer.

This is a Grass of the Leopard strain. The pattern on the tail should have rounded spots not jagged ones.

A nicely shaped Leopard female. A rounded tail and a colorless appearance are to be desired.

This is the ever-popular Blue Grass guppy. The fine, small spots and the light white-blue coloration make this a magnificent fish.

This fish is the same lineage as the one on the right. Unfortunately the dorsal is short, but that is attractive in this strain which, hopefully, might soon be fixed.

A new type of Grasstail with a metallic blue across the whole body.

A Grasstail with some Leopard blood. The tail is too small in this fish.

A new type produced from the Blue Grass. There is a lot of Neon Tuxedo blood in this fish.

This is the Russian Tuxedo. It hardly competes with the Japanese strain. Photo by Viktor Datzkevich.

In contests, the Leopard is judged in the Grass category, but since it is a line that has been around for a long time, I would like to see it supported as an independent strain.

One virtually never sees Golden or Albino Leopards, perhaps because their lineages are hard to support.

Long Fin types seem to be being maintained, but the facts that their fins are losing their white color and their bodies are becoming smaller are worrisome.

This flashy guppy is a Mosaic Tuxedo. It was produced by a cross between a Mosaic and a Tuxedo.

Tuxedo

This name was given because the lower half of the body is a dark color, making the fish look like it is wearing a tuxedo. Along with its tuxedo body, the special characteristic of this type is that its dorsal is wide, large and long compared to other varieties.

Tuxedo is a dominant trait, so you can produce numerous types by crossbreeding with it.

GERMAN YELLOW TUXEDO. Introduced in 1969 from Germany, this strain has dorsal and caudal fins of an elegant silk-like tint. One can indeed appreciate the beautiful taste of German aquarists. In order to maintain this strain's characteristic, its spotless green-yellow caudal fin, mating with close relatives has been emphasized. As a result, we are seeing deformities and abnormalities as well as decreased fecundity.

From now on, selective breeding must be conducted not only on the basis of outward appearance, but also on improving the physical constitution of the fish. Fans of German Yellow breeding are increasing in number, so we look forward to such a change.

MOSAIC TUXEDO. The Mosaic Tuxedo's lower body is a deep navy blue or green and the root of the dorsal fin down to the root of the caudal shows whitish coloration. The dorsal fin is large, long and beautiful. The caudal fin is a wide Delta with a Mosaic design. This is a variety that attracts attention with the contrast between the Tuxedo body and the flashy caudal fin.

NEON TUXEDO. This is a domesticized strain from the imported Neon Tuxedo. It shows silver hues on its back and its caudal is a Delta tail. It is thought to have been produced by mating a Red

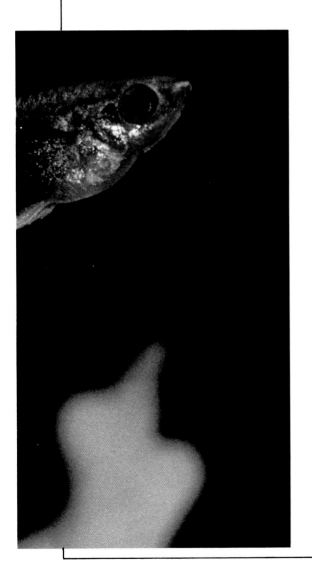

A German Yellow is considered the peak of achievement. This is a Tuxedo with a caudal fin like a white silken scarf.

The body of this German Yellow has grown larger through selective breeding. This is a wonderful specimen.

The tail of this Mosaic Tuxedo female displays the same design as Mosaic males.

This is the same strain as the fish to the right. The goal in the selective breeding of this strain is to produce a pale-colored Mosaic Tuxedo.

A type of Tuxedo produced by crossbreeding a German Yellow with a Mosaic Tuxedo.

A magnificent Longfinned Tuxedo with a desirable black edge on its tail. This characteristic has never been fixed.

A Longfin Redtail Tuxedo. Not suitable for breeding because of the malformed gonopodium (anal fin).

A domestically raised (Japanese) Redtail Tuxedo. In most of the world this fish is a Black Tuxedo Flamingo.

A domestically raised (Japanese) Neon Tuxedo. It is a strong, beautiful specimen with a silver dorsal fin.

A magnificent long dorsal Mosaic Tuxedo beautifully offset against the Water Sprite.

A German Yellow Tuxedo female. Maintaining any strain requires having proven females as the absolute necessity for breeding.

A beautiful Green Tuxedo produced from the German Yellow Tuxedo.

This is a top quality contemporary specimen of a Tuxedo with a beautiful caudal fin.

A group of German Black Tuxedos. Photographed in Germany by Burkhard Kahl.

Tuxedo with a Neon Guppy. For this reason, when you get babies, they definitely show Red Tuxedo characteristics.

Other types domesticated from imported Tuxedos are the RED TAIL TUXEDO, LEOPARD TUXEDO, BLACK TUXEDO, etc. These are sleek in shape and their round tipped caudals are unusual for Delta tails. Strains like these among imports are, as a whole, unpopular now.

GOLDEN TUXEDOS are not often produced, just to the extent that Red Tail Tuxedos are.

As for ALBINO TUXEDOS, NEON TUXEDO, RED TAIL TUXEDO and other types, their silver backs are lovely. These are very popular types with names like ALBINO SILVER BRONZE TUXEDO, but they are very difficult to maintain.

An attractive German Yellow with a cream colored tail.

Young American Flamingo Tuxedos, also referred to as Three-quarter Blacks with a Red Delta tail. Photo by A. Roth.

Blue Tuxedos, called in America: "Blue Delta Tail Half Black". Photo at the Mac Guppy Hatchery. In the 1950-1970 era, America was the prime supplier of good guppies. Then Singapore took over the lead and has maintained it ever since, probably because they have much better live foods and cheaper labor to select good fish from amongst the large spawns of guppies.

The Russians have produced this intense red and purple Tuxedo. It has a moderately long but proud dorsal fin. Photo by Anatoly Noznov, Moscow, USSR.

This is a complete brood, fully matured, of a Half Black (Tuxedo) strain produced in Germany and photographed by Burkhard Kahl.

This purple Tuxedo has good dorsal length and a nicely shaped body. It is one of the famous Hahnel strains of the 1960's. Photo by Dr. Herbert R. Axelrod.

Another purple Tuxedo. The black on the body doesn't produce enough Tuxedo, but you can see where the strain was in 1976. Photo by Dr. Herbert R. Axelrod.

The early beginnings of the Delta tail guppy produced in Florida. Photo by Dr. Herbert R. Axelrod.

RIGHT: A lovely metallic Red Tuxedo, greatly admired by the Japanese. Photographed by Dr. Herbert R. Axelrod in 1976.

BELOW: A pair of early (1978) Tuxedos. At that time emphasis in America was simply on warm, pastel colors, a darkened caudal peduncle, and as much color in the female as possible.

The purple snakeskin Tuxedo, an American strain of 1976. Photo by Dr. Herbert R. Axelrod.

This Tuxedo snakeskin male has major faults according to today's standards. The faults include a skinny body, unmatched tail and dorsal patterns, and bad dorsal coloring.

This four-month old male American Tuxedo, or Half-black as it was called then, won championship after championship. Photo by Dr. Herbert R. Axelrod (1976).

ABOVE:This was a champion guppy strain called a Flamingo Tuxedo. It won a first prize at the Florida Tropical Fish Farmers Show in 1986. It would be a great fish if the dorsal matched the tail. Photo by Dr. Harry Grier.

RIGHT:This Halfblack, or Tuxedo, was produced and photographed by Dr. Eduard Schmidt-Focke in 1967. Dr. Schmidt-Focke tried to produce an all black guppy and an all black Betta.

Others

SWORD Tail. Those fishes whose upper caudal extends in a long filament are called Top Swords; those whose lower part extends are called Bottom Swords; and those with both sections extending are known as Double Swords. Each type has a reliable genealogy and is called a variety, but generally they are not very popular and are raised only by a specific segment of guppy lovers. Furthermore, each has its own Golden and Albino, beautiful in its own way but not in the same way as generally is true of other strains.

MONOCHROME. There are single-color caudal fin versions of every type, but only the Albino Red Tail and the Golden (called the Flamingo) enjoy any popularity; it seems as though the other types are not being maintained.

TIGER. This an adorable type: its body is a thin sepia color, its scales are rimmed in black, the body has red, yellow, and green coloring; and the top of the head and tip of the nose are black. Several years ago this variety was restored. Using a Bottom Sword as a base, it was crossbred with a Grass Tail, King Cobra, Mosaic, and others, producing a wide variety of strains.

This Bottom Sword guppy was bred in Austria and won first prize in a 1968 show. Photo by Dr. Karl Knaack.

At the same Viennese show, this Double Sword took first prize in Vienna. Photo by Dr. Karl Knaack.

Midge Hill photographed this magnificent American Double Sword guppy.

In 1964 the East German author and artist, Hans Frey, depicted the various guppy strains: going counterclockwise, the top fish is a Pointed tail, a Fantail, a Delta tail, a Top Sword, a Double Sword and a "fancy" female with color in her dorsal fin.

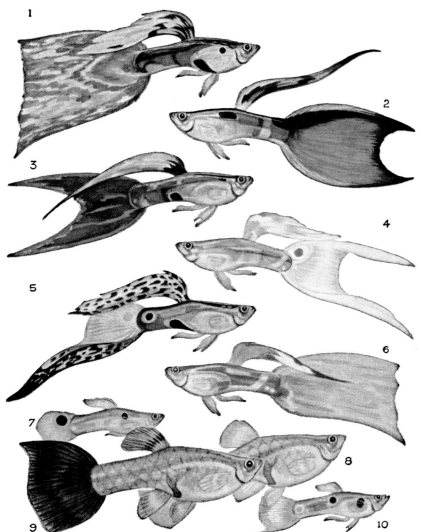

A Bottom Sword. Photo by Dr. Herbert R. Axelrod.

A Lacetail Top Sword. Photo by Dr. Herbert R. Axelrod.

American Guppies of the 1960's from Paul Hahnel's stocks: 1. Veiltail. 2. Betta Tail. 3. Scissors Tail. 4. Golden Double Swordtail. 5. Leopard, Bottom Sword. 6. Albino, Scarftail. 7. Common Wild type. 8. Gold female. 9. Pointed Tail female. 10. Common Wild Swordtail. This drawing from ALL ABOUT GUPPIES by Dr. Leon Whitney and Paul Hahnel.

Lyretail Guppy. Photo by Dr. Herbert R. Axelrod.

1. Lyretail Guppy. 2. Wild pintails. 3. Bottom Sword. 4. Bottom Sword. 5. Tuxedo Bottom Sword. 6. Flamingo Bottom Sword. 7. Rainbow Bottom Sword. 8. Leopard Cobra Bottom Sword.

A blue Bottom Sword with a touch of wild coloring. These are ideal to keep together in a school in a dedicated aquarium.

A vigorously healthy Bottom Sword. The monocle design on the flank provides a nice accent.

This is the old standard Bottom Sword. Occasionally Double Swords similar to this appear.

A Bottom Sword thought to be of the Grass strain. The color and design on the sword is very distinctive.

A Double Sword wild-type guppy. This is especially attractive when they appear as a school of fish.

A red Double Sword with magnificent body color. This is a hearty specimen.

A beautiful pastel-colored Longfin Bottom Sword of very high quality.

A Longfin blue Bottom Sword. This ribbon-type Bottom Sword is very unusual.

A Longfin Lace Bottom Sword. The Lace design is very distinctive.

A Longfin Bottom Sword of the Grass strain. This is a strain which has proven very difficult to fix.

Characteristics of Females by Variety

It is often said that females are hard to select compared to males. This is because, whereas males are judged by external appearance, with females you often do not even know if they are true specimens of a given strain. Deformed or abnormal females are beside the point, but given that the female's basic function is reproduction, it is critical that you choose a fertile female that will accurately transmit the magnificent qualities of the male. Your choice of a female can easily sway your results.

It is often said that a roundtailed colorless female is best. However, this does not mean that the same standards apply to all females. When a type becomes established as a strain, to a certain extent the markings on the female seem to fade, as they do on the male.

Let me speak about the basic lineages by variety and their caudal fin shapes and designs, and their body markings.

Mosaic

Compared to females of other varieties, the Mosaic female's body is rather large. The caudal fin is large overall and the upper portion is larger still. It is a faint blue or yellow color with a pale flame design. On a good specimen, the design is unbroken from the top to the bottom of the fin. The dorsal fin is not very big and is sometimes spotted.

This magnificent female bred true. The males were mainly Double Swords or Lyretails. Photo by Ruda Zukal of a Czechoslovakian strain.

Previously illustrated Cobra female.

Previously illustrated female Mosaic.

A beautifully balanced pair of golden Cobras or Snakeskins. This is an American breed. Photo by Dr. Herbert R. Axelrod.

King Cobra

Variations abound in the King Cobra family, so I will address only the major points.

The female King Cobra has a rounded caudal with a somewhat elongated upper section. On the caudal are faint ink blotches and spots. Females with entirely black caudals are not desirable.

The Lace Cobra female has a rounded unpatterned tail. However, as its reliability increases, a thin lace design appears on the caudal at the root.

The Mosaic Cobra female looks very much like the Mosaic female; from outward appearances you can barely tell them apart.

Grass

There are many different strains in this family: Glass Grass, Grass Grass, Blue Grass, the Leopard Grass which resulted from crossbreeding with the Leopard, and others.

Previously illustrated Grass female.

Previously illustrated Grasstail female.

Previously illustrated Tiger Bottom Sword female.

Previously illustrated Leopard female.

A German Yellow Tuxedo female, previously illustrated.

Ideally, the Grass female has a rounded, unfig-ured caudal, but in reality you hardly ever see that kind of female. Most usually have a faint ink pattern and/or spots. Those with Mosaic blood have a slightly elongated upper caudal section. Females with rounded or egg-shaped caudal fins are best.

Leopard

The best females in this group have rounded, patternless tails. Since crossbreeding with the King Cobra often is carried out to maintain the Leopard genealogy, the upper and lower sections of the caudal have become slightly blackened. If mated with the Grass, the tail is rounded but inky.

A well marked, but poorly shaped, female thought to carry the Leopard markings, but she failed to produce many good males and this strain disappeared from American breeders. Photo by Dr. Herbert R. Axelrod.

A Tuxedo female giving birth. Photo by Ruda Zukal. LEFT: Many aquarists test their female guppies by adding the male hormone testosterone to the water. The female takes on male characteristics and color, thus showing what kind of genes they may carry. Usually females treated with male hormones are useless in further breeding. Photo by Dr. Herbert R. Axelrod.

Tuxedo

The German Yellow has a pale, glossy Tuxedo design on its body with a gold-covered caudal fin.

Specimens with no pattern but black dabs are not to be preferred.

As for Neon Tuxedos, females with a thin, glossy Tuxedo body and a caudal fin that appears blue if viewed against the light are best. Females with shining metallic blue caudals that look Neon Tuxedo-ish produce many Red Tail Tuxedos.

Sword Tail

Females of this group have unfigured, round caudal fins. If you select females of this sort, you can support the Sword Tail genealogy using only one aquarium.

Albino

When mating two Albinos, the best females are not white, but rather as yellow as possible. Furthermore, it is easier to get Albino babies when mating with grape-eyed females than with red-eyed ones.

Long Fin

As long as the fins have beautiful extension and spread, it is fine to use the same criteria as with any variety to select a female of pure lineage.

A Top Sword wild type of guppy with his mate. Photo by Gene Wolfsheimer.

LEFT: A previously illustrated pair of Albino Mosaics.

BELOW: A Golden Albino (lutino) female, well marked. This is an established strain from East Germany. Photo by Hans Joachim Richter. This female is delivering a baby tail first. Sometimes they come out head first.

What is an Albino?

Albino is the generic name for the unique white strain in which the black-colored body pigment (melanin) is lacking. Albinos exist as a strain in all the basic varieties: Albino Grass, Albino Cobra, etc. However, Mosaics and Tuxedos do not breed well with Albinos so those lines are difficult to maintain.

Albinos often represent whiteness, but in reality there are yellow and pink Albinos as well as white. This phenomenon results from the degree of albinism. With pure Albinos, the eyes are red and the body is a white color with a pinkish tint. Specimens with yellowish bodies and grape-colored eyes are also Albinos. Ordinarily the former are called "red eyes" and the latter "grape-eyes."

Golden female guppies. They are not albino. Photo by Dr. Herbert R. Axelrod.

The Russians produced this magnificent strain of Golden Snakeskins. The females are highly colored, perhaps being the most colorful strain of female guppies yet fixed. Photo by H. Kyselov.

Albinism is caused by the lack of an enzyme called tyrosinase or by a blocking of that enzyme's effectiveness. Tyrosinase is an enzyme that produces melanin by oxidizing tyrosine. Melanin produces body colors from brown to black. If melanin is lacking, it is only natural that albinism should result.

The phenomenon of albinism is born in the genes. The albino gene, the product of a mutation, is recessive.

An F_1 born of crossbreeding with a specimen of normal pigmentation will have an Albino gene even though it looks normal. The F_2 born of two of these F_1 should be divided by a 3:1 ratio into normally pigmented and Albino pigmented offspring. If two F_2 Albinos are mated, all Albinos will be born. In this way, if you have one Albino, many can be produced in a matter of months, at least theoretically.

A young Albino Red Tail with a large dorsal fin. The red on the tail is impressive.

An Albino King Cobra with a beautifully patterned tail. This is an excellent specimen.

An Albino King Cobra covered beautifully with the
Cobra design throughout its entire body.

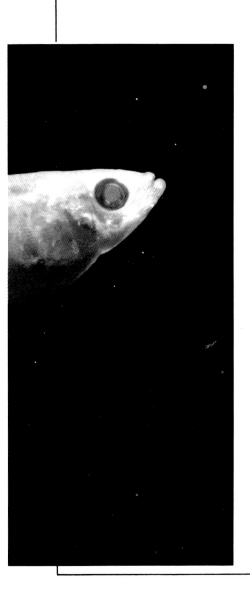

This Albino King Cobra is a very popular strain, but it
is very difficult to maintain as a true-breeding strain.

An Albino Grass with a magnificent sheen.

The Albino Mosaic is difficult to breed because the black part of the tail design is often missing.

A pair of Albino Mosaics. The male is dancing before the female prior to mating.

The Albino Bottom Sword is often used in selective breeding because it carries a strong albino gene.

An Albino Red Tail Tuxedo. This type is distinguished from the normal Red Tail by its basic color pattern.

The Albino Red Tail is a very flashy fish. The large tail is a perfect Delta type.

An Albino Grass female. Albinos of yellow body coloration seem to be more robust than those which are white.

An Albino Grass of pre-eminent style. It is difficult to get a spawn from albinos with perfectly red eyes like this one.

An Albino Mosaic Cobra female. The coloration and design of the caudal fin are distinctive.

A very rare Albino Mosaic King Cobra. The pattern on the tail is interesting but the shape of the tail leaves something to be desired.

An Albino produced from a Blue Mosaic. The pale color of the dorsal and caudal fins is lovely.

An Albino from a Neon Tuxedo. This is a lovely fish with an overall silver sheen.

Albinos have rather weak constitutions and do not breed very hardily. It is not unusual to find males with little procreative power or females that cannot conceive. Further, to support the lineage is not easy, since litters are small even if conception does occur. F_2 and F_3 are your real focus, and it often happens that you cannot get any offspring at all in these generations. For this reason, aquarists always crossbreed Albinos with regular strains, producing an F_1 that possesses an Albino gene, taking some Albinos in F_2, mating those Albinos with each other, and then crossing those offspring with regular strains. Thus, the Albino genealogy is maintained by crossbreeding to get back to the original.

An interesting breeding point is that if you mate an Albino with a Golden, a specimen of regular variety having an Albino gene appears. You should definitely give this a try.

Wild-type pintail guppies produced in American hatcheries in the 1960's. Photo by Dr. Herbert R. Axelrod.

Hints About Selective Breeding and Guppy Fin Shapes

When most people look quickly at a guppy, what they immediately notice are coloration and caudal fin shape. Strictly speaking, you should look at the entire specimen: dorsal fin, caudal fin, body shape, coloration, size, etc. But, generally the caudal catches the eye first.

Various Tail Shapes Recognized in Japan

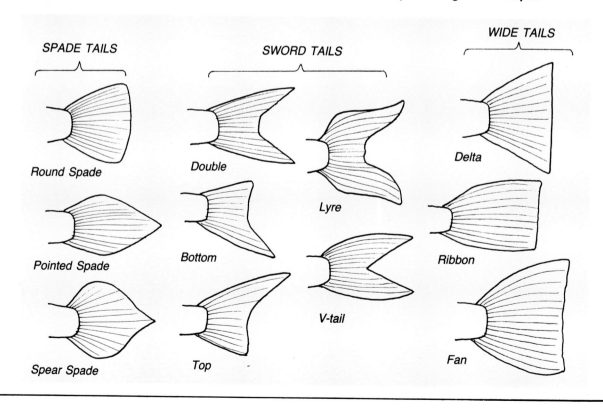

SPADE TAILS

Round Spade

Pointed Spade

Spear Spade

SWORD TAILS

Double

Bottom

Top

Lyre

V-tail

WIDE TAILS

Delta

Ribbon

Fan

The wild types are types for which selective breeding has not advanced much. The representative type is the Round Tail, having a naturally occurring rounded fin that is not very large. Variations on the Round Tail include, among others, the Pin Tail where the tail abruptly extends into a pin-like shape and the Spade Tail where the caudal is shaped like the spade on playing cards. Wild types are lovely types that swim vigorously around the aquarium, but these days they do not seem to be very popular.

Next is the Sword Tail type; and as the name indicates, these have tails that extend like swords. The basic strains are the Top Sword, where the upper caudal extends, and the Bottom Sword, where the lower part of the tail is elongated. Variations include the Double Sword, with extensions on both the upper and lower parts of the caudal, and the Lyre Tail, with a tail shaped like a harp. Sword Tail types have possessed a combination of beauty and vigor since the original sword-shaped caudal fin were established. A group of Sword Tails is nicely suited to an aquarium with lots of plant growth. On the whole, this type has a long life span. It is quite common with these fish that their caudal sections will be fully elongated within six months of birth and that they live for more than one year.

The popular current these days is to favor the Bell Tail, the Fan Tail, and the large, widespreading Long Tail types. The last comes from advanced selective breeding with the Delta Tail.

From the mid 1950s until about 1960 the Bell Tail type was popular. Imported from the United States, this type had a long dorsal fin and a beautiful body. However, excessive close breeding within the same line resulted in feebleness and, after several years, the type degenerated.

The Fan Tail, with its caudal that opens like a Japanese folding fan, appeared as a bit of ornamentation on the fancy guppy. The Fan Tail spreads very nicely; it is flashy and worth seeing.

The Delta Tail, today the most common shape, was produced when the Fan Tail underwent selec-

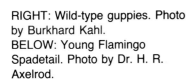

RIGHT: Wild-type guppies. Photo by Burkhard Kahl.
BELOW: Young Flamingo Spadetail. Photo by Dr. H. R. Axelrod.

tive breeding. In Japan, we use the name Delta Tail. As its name suggests, the Delta Tail suggests a three-sided shape. Most contemporary guppy strains are Delta or Fan Tail. For this reason, the name of a strain will not be "such and such Delta" or "such and such Fan Tail"; instead, strain names are given by color, design, and other traits.

Recently, the Long Fin type, also called the Swallow, has been extremely popular. This is a type that established the mutation of each fin extending irregularly. Females with their long extended fins look beautiful and elegant.

You cannot get a litter from mating a Long Fin male and a Long Fin female. This is because the gonopodium (the male reproductive organ) is so long as to inhibit appropriate functioning. In order to preserve the Long Fin strain, it is absolutely necessary to crossbreed Long Fin specimens with fish of regular varieties that have a Long Fin gene.

However, for the "Ribbon" Long Fin variety, you cross a Long Fin female with a regular male to get Ribbon types in F_1.

If you think about selective breeding from the perspective of caudal fin shape, you can imagine a German Yellow Long Fin and other not-yet-produced Long Fin types. You can also imagine a King Cobra or Tuxedo Sword Tail type; the combination of an Albino or a Golden with a Long Fin, etc. If you think about it, there is no end to the possibilities.

You should definitely set some goals for yourself and accept the challenge of selective breeding.

A violet, purple Longfin from Austria. Photo by Dr. Karl Knaack.

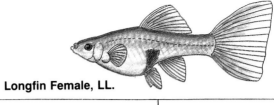

Longfin Female, LL.

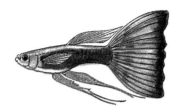

Longfin Male, LL
Unable to breed.

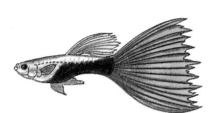

Normal Longfin, NL
Able to breed.

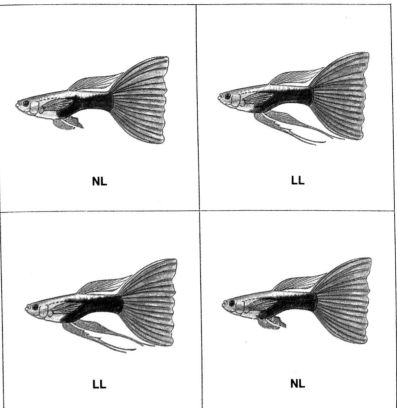

BREEDING THE LONGFIN GUPPY. SECOND GENERATION, F$_2$.
You must start with a Longfin female whose chromosomes are labelled LL. You cannot use a male longfin, LL, because he is unable to copulate due to his misshapen anal fin (gonopodium). You must use a Longfin Normal, NL, with some genes for Longfin. The males you produce will be about 50% Normal Longfins, NL, and 50% pure Longfins, LL. You can only get Normal Longfins as a second generation, as shown above.

P
Parental Generation

♀ albino $\frac{a}{a}$ ✕ ♂ wild $\frac{A}{A}$

F₁
1st Daughter Generation
100% wild

♀ wild $\frac{A}{a}$ ✕ ♂ wild $\frac{A}{a}$

F₂ (3:1)
2nd Daughter Generation: 75% wild: A/A or A/a (25% A/A and 50% A/a)

25% albino: a/a

Crossing of a homozygous albino female with a homozygous wild-colored male guppy. Symbols: **P** = parental generation, **F₁** = first daughter generation, **F₂** = second daughter generation.

BREEDING TECHNIQUE

The Life Cycle of Domestic Guppies

The life span of guppies today averages one year, although it varies by strain. Among strains developed through selective breeding, specimens that live more than one year are rare; thus, guppies are generally thought of as one year fish.

Short life cycle in guppies may be caused by the raising of the fish or the way in which or purpose for which selective breeding is carried out. Unbalanced diet invites deformity or nutritional difficulties; raising the fish in warm water quickens growth but it also shortens life expectancy.

With selective breeding, the all important points of health and vigor are easily forgotten when attention concentrates on color, design, and caudal fin size. Selective breeding that casually crosses this and that is problematic. When all is said and done, an orthodox approach to raising guppies and a systematic breeding program are desirable; that is, balanced feeding, a slightly lower water temperature of 22 to 24 degrees centigrade, and mating specimens from strains that are already established to some extent.

Guppies become full grown after going through several stages: as baby fish for three or four weeks after birth until the gonopodium of the male develops; as juvenile fish until about two months after birth when the caudal fin enlarges and the basic colorations take on clarity; as adolescent fish until three or four months after birth; and as full grown fish after six months. Nonetheless, guppies are known as precocious fish because their reproductive capability develops about three weeks after birth. It is not inaccurate to say that after one month passes most males are able to reproduce. Males and females are separated after three weeks in order to allow you to obtain virgin females. This is absolutely necessary if you intend to carry out selective breeding.

If growth goes normally, after about two months the caudal fin shape, color, and design are clarified and you can anticipate future development in this area. The adolescent period, three to four months from birth, is the most active period in the life cycle, a time when you can appreciate the beauty of healthy, lively movement in your guppies. Then,

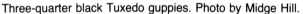

Three-quarter black Tuxedo guppies. Photo by Midge Hill.

at six months or so, the fish reaches the peak of its beauty. When it passes seven months, degeneration suddenly sets in. The luster disappears from the body; the caudal fin splits; movement becomes lethargic. If you continue to give your guppies high level care even after this, the specimens will live to about one year, but in most cases when the guppies lose their beauty their owners put them in mixed tanks and treat them carelessly, so they die. Since these are the guppies that have given you so much pleasure, you want to treat them well even after they are past their prime. A guppy that has been forgotten is an unhappy guppy.

The female guppy is about the same size as the male until about three months. After that, she rapidly grows larger. The female all at once grows larger especially after having borne her first litter. Compared to the male, the female is plain in terms of form and coloration, but she bears the critical burden of passing on the qualities of the male to the next generation. It is not necessarily the case that a specimen with a large body and big caudal fin is a good female. Rather than outward appearance, the effective transmission of dominant characteristics makes a female magnificent.

If you do not separate male and female specimens in a litter early on, they will procreate after about two months. The first litter will be about ten babies. If the female is a healthy one, she will bear another litter after a twenty to twenty five day cycle. The Albino and the Long Fin types do not require this period. This suggests one possible reason why they lose their reproductive power as selective breeding proceeds.

A beautiful, healthy female bears young in accordance with her regular cycle. This suggests that "healthy and fertile" is an important theme for future selective breeding efforts.

Selection and Purchase of the Seed Fish

If you aim to produce good offspring, the most important factor is the selection of the parents. Unless you have a special reason in mind, you want to put emphasis on confirmation of family line rather than on outward appearance. A fish that is systematically bred is the most appropriate specimen for the seed fish because it has undergone a severe selection and weeding out process in order to ensure that it sufficiently exhibits the particular characteristics of the various strains that have been crossed.

Among guppies born of well-pedigreed seed fish, most become good quality fish resembling the parents. However, sometimes the job of producing a good fish is not brought to completion after birth; there may be problems in environment or methods of raising the fish, such as care of the fish, diet, and water management. By contrast, the possibility of obtaining good fish from parent spec-

A mixed tank of Swordtail guppies from America. Photographed at the Mac Guppy Hatchery.

A mixed tank of fancy guppies. This type of tank is offered in many German petshops which do NOT specialize in guppies. Photo by Burkhard Kahl.

In order to preserve the virginity of females, a net within the guppy tank can be used to isolate those females which you plan to breed. Drawn by John Quinn.

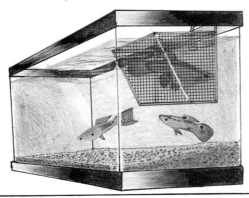

imens of bad lineage is slim. Even if unusually beautiful fish appear, many will have short life spans or no reproductive capacity. When offspring can be produced by such seed fish, there are many deformities and infirmities, and the line does not continue.

With male guppies, their caudal fin size, color and design always tend to catch the eye, but you want to choose a specimen that has a strong form, thick caudal peduncle, and good overall physical balance; and importantly, one that swims energetically and actively pursues females. As for females, it is important that they display the particular characteristics of caudal fin shape, coloration, and design of their respective strains. Furthermore, since you want a minimum of one litter, you want to select a female whose abdominal region is sufficiently expanded and blackened.

Regarding when to purchase the seed fish, young specimens three to five months old are preferable. With fish younger than this you will be unable to evaluate their quality as adults. Also, once six months has passed the fish becomes difficult to use in breeding; furthermore, the specimens remain pretty for only a short time beyond six months, so you are not able to enjoy viewing them for long.

Many types of guppies are sold in tropical fish shops, but prices and quality are certainly not consistent. If you consider reliability of lineage, an established strain is more expensive; however, you can also regard them as cheaper in the long run because an established strain produces larger litters. There are also fish that are high-priced because they are unusual, regardless of the degree of establishment. Fish prices are largely determined by supply and demand, so the buyer has to make his selection after considering how he would like to enjoy them later.

You will probably not go wrong if you buy your guppies in a shop that has several different varieties in stock, each in some volume, and if you inquire about lineage and reliability before making the purchase.

Caring for Spawn and Juvenile Fish

When the fertilized eggs ripen, the female's abdomen swells and the lower portion turns black. When these so-called marks of pregnancy appear, the female will exhibit behavior different from usual, for instance, swimming at the edge of the aquarium, at the top, or on the bottom. This is evidence that the time to give birth is near. Around this time, if you look at the female's blackish lower abdomen you can discern the spawn and their big eyes inside the eggs.

It is best to separate a female in this condition from the male if your aquarium facilities permit, for to the female, who becomes quite sensitive as birth approaches, there is no merit in being in the same tank with the male. If the female is chased around by the male, she may become hysterical and jump out of the tank. When you confirm that fertilization has taken place, remove the female and keep her separate from the male. When birth

approaches, put her in a spawning tank or spawning box and collect the babies from there. However, if it is the first pregnancy, the female may give birth without becoming very large. Thus, rather than judging from the swelling of the stomach, it is more accurate to anticipate spawning by counting days from the time of mating. Ordinarily, the female will give birth approximately one month after having been impregnated by the male.

If you do not separate males and females but raise them in the same tank, the female may bear her first litter as early as two months after birth. Furthermore, a female who has been impregnated one time can bear three separate litters even if she has no more contact with males. In the case of Albinos, however, by the third litter many females release half eggs and with half spawn. When this happens, the female must be impregnated again or else another litter will not be born.

The length of time between litters depends greatly on on water temperature and on the strain. The size of the litter varies by strain and lineage, but a young female's first litter is usually about ten fish, the second, twenty to thirty, and the third, thirty to fifty. There are also varieties like the German Yellow Tuxedo which produce only one litter of a few fish. In between these types are those where the female bears only one litter but of nearly one hundred babies. Yet, we cannot say that a large litter is necessarily better.

For giving birth, a spawning tank or a spawning box is used. In the spawning tank, it is best to create a relaxed environment for the female with lots of water plants. Use new water and raise the temperature about two degrees centigrade above normal; this acts as a stimulus and the female will drop her litter within one to two days. The lush grasses become a perfect hideaway for the young, but the female will sometimes eat her young right after giving birth to them. Albinos in particular are prone to this kind of behavior, perhaps because they have poor vision or perhaps because the body coloration of the young resembles food.

A spawning box is a simple, easy-to-use piece of equipment. If you put the female in it too early, however, she will become stressed; watch the timing and move her to the box a day or so before she gives birth. When birth is over, immediately remove the parent fish and give the babies plenty of room.

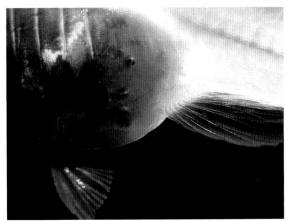

A female of Golden lineage with a well-rounded abdomen indicating that birth is close at hand. Guppies breed about once a month.

The mark of pregnancy is visible on this young female.

Baby guppies about one week old. If they are fed brine shrimp they will grow very quickly.

The moment of birth. The baby fish come out in a rounded shape; then they quickly swim away.

Lively, active swimming is one of the main attractions of guppies. A young Grass male is shown chasing a female.

A female should be moved to a separate tank and allowed to rest sufficiently after dropping her litter. You should give careful consideration to whether or not you want to produce another litter from that female. Be sure to consider your own aquarium facilities—even if babies are produced you might not be able to house them.

For the fry, body development is the most important aspect of the first three weeks after birth. It is especially necessary that food be divided into several feedings per day. Just hatched brine shrimp are the perfect food in that they have good nutritional balance and do not foul the water. When using a spawning box, keep the babies there for ten days and use a siphon to remove excretions and uneaten food particles so the water does not turn bad. After that, move the babies into a ten gallon tank—here, a large aquarium is not necessary.

A guppy being born tail first.
Photo by Hans Joachim Richter.

Baby guppies which have been surgically removed from a dying mother. These fish were able to live. Photo by Arend van den Nieuwenhuizen.

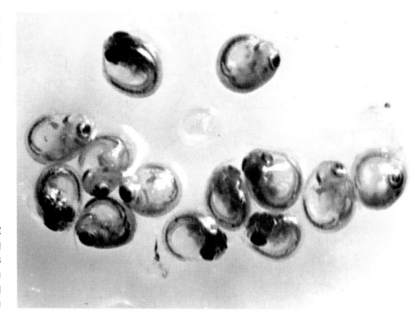

BELOW: Some mothers are not very maternal and eat their offspring as soon as they are born. Petshops sell special breeding traps which protect the newborn fry from being eaten. Photo by Hans Joachim Richter.

Selecting From Among the Offspring

Separate males from females at about three weeks after birth. If you are able to separate them earlier, that is even better.

Except for slow developing varieties like Albinos or the German Yellow Tuxedo, you should be able to distinguish sex after three weeks. If you cannot, it is because of abnormality or infirmity.

To distinguish guppies by sex, you can judge by body shape or by spots on the base of the male caudal fin, but the easiest method is probably to divide the specimens by the gonopodium on the males and the black lower abdomen on the females. You will be able to distinguish males from females if you put the babies in a small plastic container and examine them from the sides and bottom while applying light. At this time you should dispose of any specimens with deformities, such as bending dorsal fins, developmental abnormalities, or "needle" disease where the tips of the caudal fin become pointed.

Guppies mature quickly. If you leave fry in the same tank with the parent, the young males will begin to pursue the mother within one month after birth. A male that is so precocious usually cannot be used as a seed fish for the next generation. This is because physical growth for such fish stops midway, meaning that the specimen becomes a very small adult fish. Since these early developers cannot become seed fish, it is best to get rid of them as soon as possible. The reason males and females are separated so quickly is because guppies are such early developers; the separation is the first step in preserving virgin females for systematic selective breeding.

If you are not breeding commercially, you want to exercise deliberation in choosing males and females to parent the next generation, conducting a step-by-step selection process. In order to produce magnificent guppies, you should raise your fish in accordance with the motto, "Few in number, select in quality." Because you can manage their numbers, you can also maintain a favorable environment for the guppies. If you discover a deformed or underdeveloped specimen as you observe your fish each day, remove it as quickly as possible.

In the period from one to three months after birth, guppies undergo more changes than you would think, so there is a need to exercise caution. Fish whose colors have clearly come out and whose fins have grown after two months are good candidates for seed fish, so you want to treat them with care. You will notice at this stage sterile males and females that give an overall unbalanced look, with large bodies and small caudal fins. Dispose of these fish as soon as you discover them.

The male and the female are for the most part the same size until this time. Once you pass the three month point, the female gradually becomes larger than the male. Then, every time the female bears a litter she becomes still larger.

Select seed fish for the next generation about four months after birth, after having repeated a strict selection and weeding out process on the litter. About four months after birth is the appropriate time for mating. The offspring of young parents have the best quality. You obtain good quality babies from such parent fish in the first and second litters. If the female is healthy you may get a third or fourth litter, but in the end you will see a lot of deformities and imprecise designs on these.

The appearance in the male of the special characteristics of his strain comes about two months after birth. Around this time, body coloration and caudal fin coloration, pattern, and shape will clearly appear and you can foresee what the fish will look like when fully grown.

The Delta Tail male has a caudal fin that is straight on the top and bottom; it has angles and no curves; but when the fish is fully grown, it has a large, beautiful spread. When the caudal fin markings are pale and blurred in the center, the fish is not desirable as a seed. Also, specimens on which the tips of the caudal fin are transparent are preferable to those with blackened edges because on the latter the tip areas will remain black even when the fish attains full growth.

After the caudal, you have to give careful attention to the dorsal fin. With dorsals, a shape that conveys a sense of fullness is important. Stiff dorsal fins have no spread even when the fish grows up. In the end, both size and softness are impor-

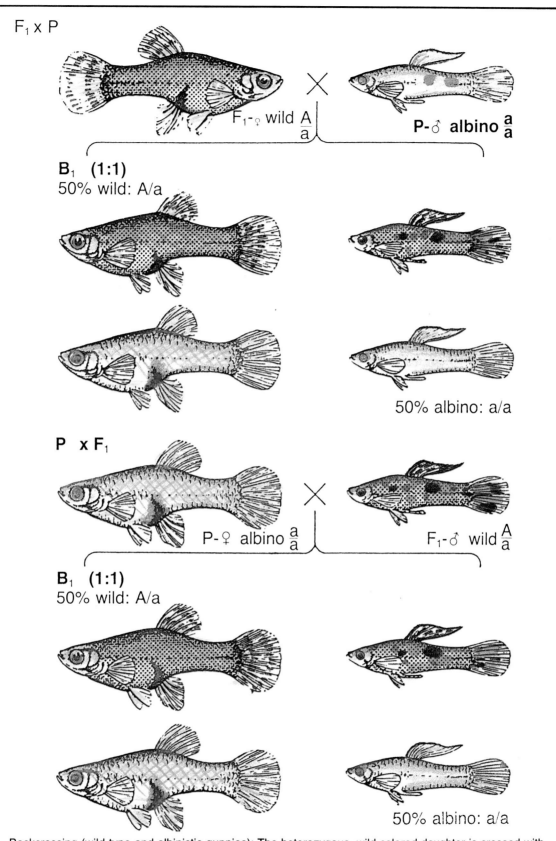

F₁ x P

F₁-♀ wild $\frac{A}{a}$ P-♂ albino $\frac{a}{a}$

B₁ (1:1)
50% wild: A/a

50% albino: a/a

P   x F₁

P-♀ albino $\frac{a}{a}$ F₁-♂ wild $\frac{A}{a}$

B₁ (1:1)
50% wild: A/a

50% albino: a/a

Backcrossing (wild-type and albinistic guppies): The heterozygous, wild-colored daughter is crossed with her homozygous, albinistic father. The progeny (**B₁** generation) consist of wild-colored and homozygous albino guppies in the proportions 1:1. The same result is achieved by reciprocal crossing: the wild-colored heterozygous son is mated with the homozygous albinistic mother.

tant with dorsals.

You definitely want to select beautiful, healthy specimens as seed fish. Deformities such as curvature of the spine, curvature of the body, and lumps have a high chance of being genetically transmitted. Deformities acquired through insufficient light or unbalanced diet are impossible to pass on genetically but you should still avoid using such specimens as parent fish.

You can evaluate the male by external appearance, but choosing the female is more difficult. It is not an exaggeration to say that the quality of the female can sway the formation of the next generation one way or another.

A magnificent female is one that is healthy and effectively passes on the qualities of the male; it is not a specimen with a large body or fins or a beautifully colored or patterned exterior. Fundamentally, a plain female with a colorless caudal fin that is not terribly large is most desirable. However, in highly established varieties there are faint designs on the caudal and spots and ink patterns may appear. When selecting the female, it is important to bear in mind that each variety has its own unique caudal fin shape and pattern.

The Meaning of F_1, F_2, and One-generation Crossbreeds

In order to conduct selective breeding to improve guppy varieties, you have to accurately understand various genetic principles and technical terms. For example, confusion often occurs between "one-generation crossbreeds" and "the first generation of a crossbreed" and between F_1 and F_2 versus a first and second litter.

The Mosaic Cobra is a first generation hybrid born of crossbreeding a King Cobra male with a red Mosaic female. Even if F_1 and F_2 are mated within the litter, they reproduce without abnormalities or feebleness appearing. The genealogy is maintained by repeated mating within the same litter or by careful out-breeding.

In contrast to this, in the F_1 born of mating two different strains (a German Yellow Tuxedo male and a Tiger Bottom Sword female) wonderful silverbacked Red Tail Tuxedos are produced. However, this type is extremely weak and the F_2 from intra-litter breeding is even more feeble, often dying out before they are fully grown. This sort of phenomenon in which the F_1 born of mating different varieties cannot produce F_2 is called a one-generation crossbreed.

A female Tuxedo guppy and her newborn. Photo by Ruda Zukal.

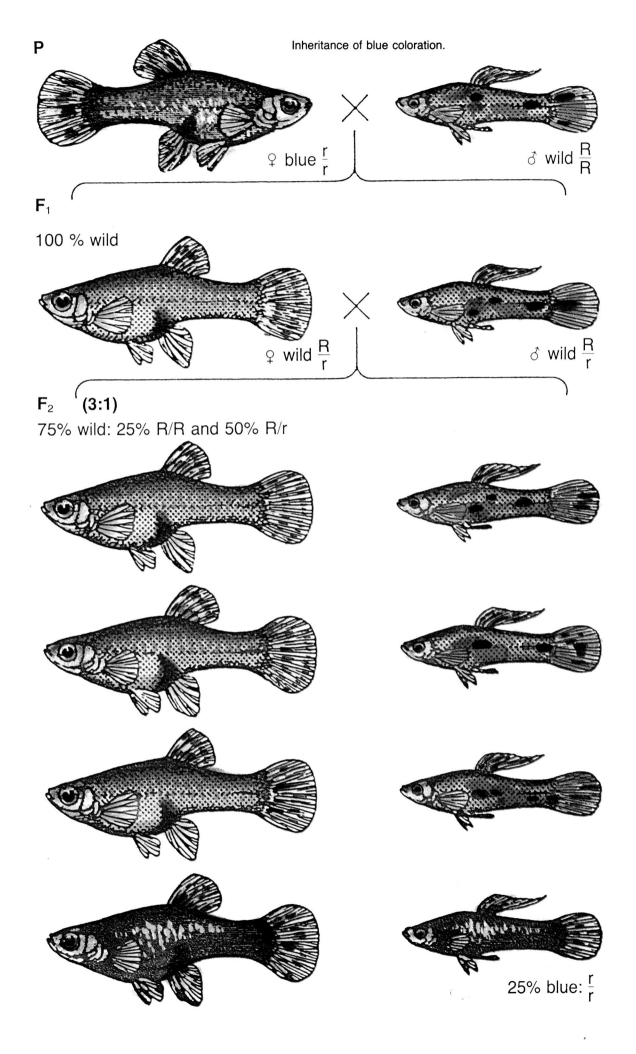

P

Inheritance of blue coloration.

♀ blue $\frac{r}{r}$ × ♂ wild $\frac{R}{R}$

F₁

100 % wild

♀ wild $\frac{R}{r}$ × ♂ wild $\frac{R}{r}$

F₂ (3:1)

75% wild: 25% R/R and 50% R/r

25% blue: $\frac{r}{r}$

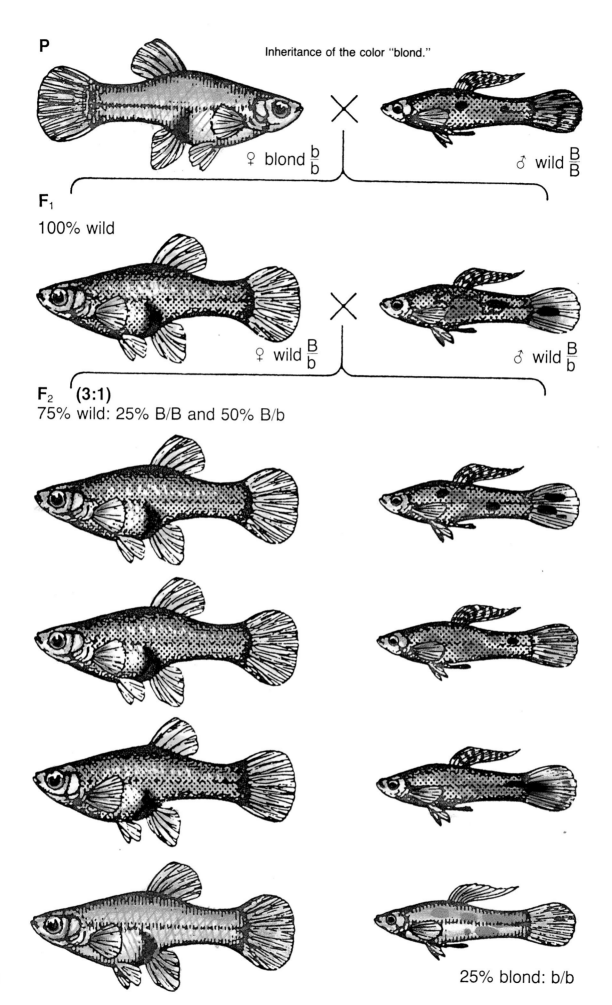

P

Inheritance of the color "blond."

♀ blond $\frac{b}{b}$ ✕ ♂ wild $\frac{B}{B}$

F₁

100% wild

♀ wild $\frac{B}{b}$ ✕ ♂ wild $\frac{B}{b}$

F₂ (3:1)

75% wild: 25% B/B and 50% B/b

25% blond: b/b

102

Special Points of Breeding

Along with selecting systematically bred, high quality seed fish, there are several other points about breeding to keep in mind to produce wonderful guppies.

In order to support a lineage, you use inbreeding. When the specimens you have selected get to be about three months old, you mate two females with one male and take the litters. You can impregnate more females, but the offspring are impossible to manage, so two females are sufficient. If you put several males and several females in one tank, you cannot know which males mated with which females. If there should be a male among the many in the tank with an unfavorable genetic trait, that might then be passed on to all the young. Even if there are a number of fish of the same high level as candidates for seed fish, choose the one that is closest to the ideal fish for the seed role. Naturally, the partners for the male should be virgin females.

As with the parents, the litter should be divided by sex about three weeks after birth. Then, repeating the process of selecting and weeding out from the litter for about three months, you are left with the male and female for the next generation. While the parent fish are still able to procreate, mate the male parent with a female offspring and the female parent with a male offspring. In this way, by closely inbreeding parent with child and specimens of the same litter with each other, you produce an established guppy strain.

If you repeat close inbreeding of the same bloodlines, harmful effects such as deformities, feeble constitution, and small size will begin to appear. These are known as the infirmities of inbreeding and usually they surface in about three years.

In order to create a new strain of guppies, you conduct outbreeding. However, actual outbreeding is mating specimens of different species. In a case such as guppies where crossbreeding takes place within the same species, interpret the term to mean crossbreeding of different varieties.

If you conduct outbreeding without going through the selection process, the type of guppy you aim to produce will likely not appear. In rare cases when magnificent specimens do emerge, most will have a short life span and be infertile. If you are able to get a litter, it will probably contain many different types, so that if you try to produce F_2 and F_3, it becomes difficult to establish the lineage. In mating different varieties, it is important that both have achieved some degree of reliability so that in crossbreeding you are only making a new hybrid of the two.

It is best to keep one aquarium for untouched females. Then, if there is an unforeseen hitch or you come into possession of an exceptional male, you always have several females ready.

Maintaining a Variety

Maintaining a variety is difficult. This section will address methods of supporting basic lineages that have long been regarded as guppy varieties (Mosaic, Grass, King Cobra, and Tuxedo) and varieties that combine assorted color variations (Golden, Albino, and Tiger) with form variations such as the Long Fin.

As mentioned previously, infirmities tied to close inbreeding emerge if you continuously mate specimens of the same litter or parents with offspring in order to establish a guppy strain. If deformities appear prior to what inbreeding would lead you to expect, they may result from problems in the selection of parent fish or failure to fully differentiate the fish's genealogy (that is, breaking down a specimen's lineage by main lineage, subordinate lineage, and so on) before mating.

In order to guard against the problems of too close inbreeding, inject new blood into the lineage. When so doing, use a specimen of a highly established strain. Then, continue to maintain the variety by repeated selecting and weeding out.

Mosaic

With the Mosaic variety, maintain a strain by breeding with other Mosaic strains. Mate offspring of the same litter in F_1, F_2, and F_3 and cross F_1 males with F_2 females and F_1 females with F_2 males. Then, through the selection and weeding out processes, the offspring come closer and closer to the standard. Select a male that has good fin spread and the same sort of dark blue or green col-

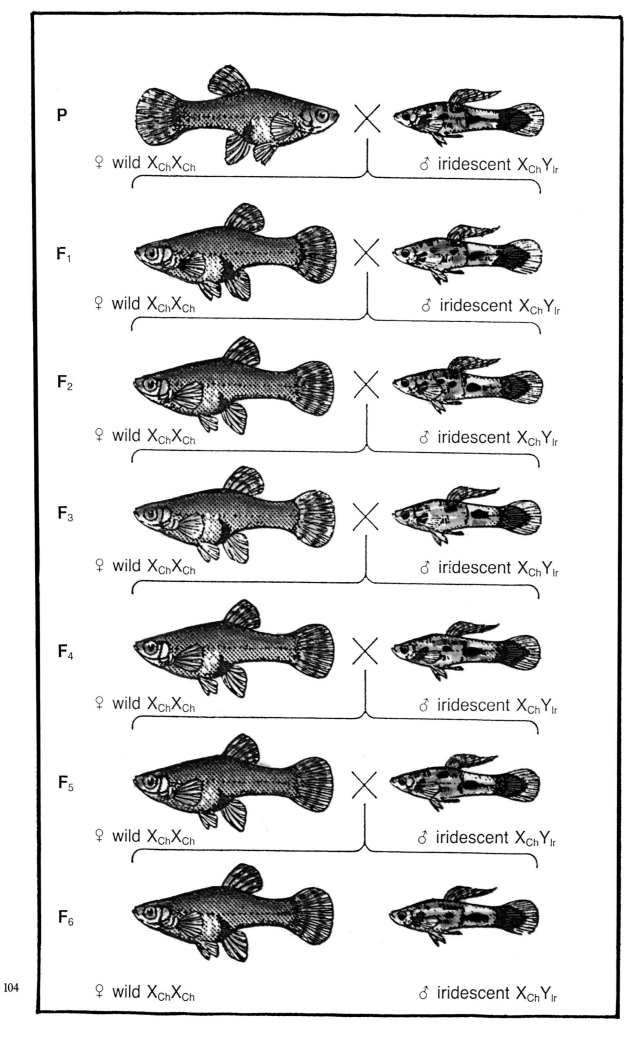

P

♀ wild $X_{Ch}X_{Ch}$ ✕   ♂ iridescent $X_{Ch}Y_{Ir}$

F₁

♀ wild $X_{Ch}X_{Ch}$ ✕   ♂ iridescent $X_{Ch}Y_{Ir}$

F₂

♀ wild $X_{Ch}X_{Ch}$ ✕   ♂ iridescent $X_{Ch}Y_{Ir}$

F₃

♀ wild $X_{Ch}X_{Ch}$ ✕   ♂ iridescent $X_{Ch}Y_{Ir}$

F₄

♀ wild $X_{Ch}X_{Ch}$ ✕   ♂ iridescent $X_{Ch}Y_{Ir}$

F₅

♀ wild $X_{Ch}X_{Ch}$ ✕   ♂ iridescent $X_{Ch}Y_{Ir}$

F₆

♀ wild $X_{Ch}X_{Ch}$ ♂ iridescent $X_{Ch}Y_{Ir}$

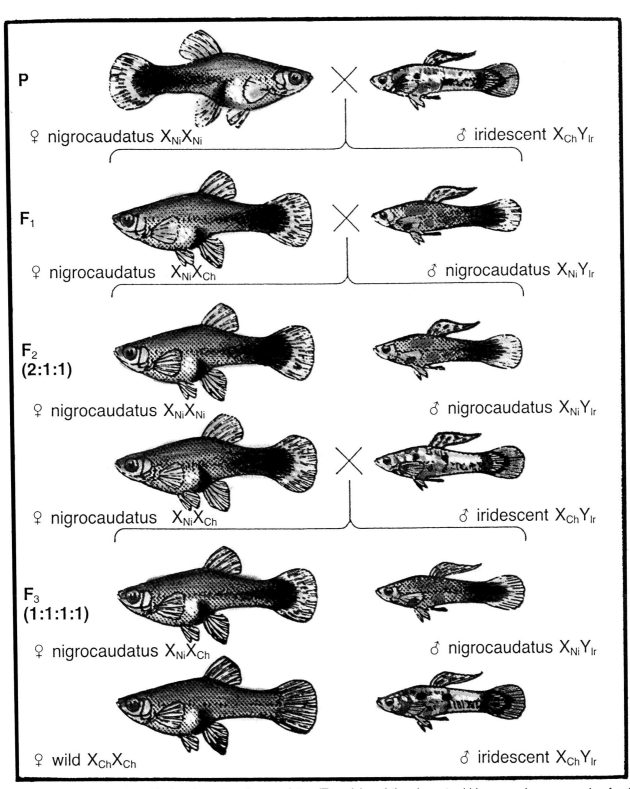

P

♀ nigrocaudatus $X_{Ni}X_{Ni}$ × ♂ iridescent $X_{Ch}Y_{Ir}$

F₁

♀ nigrocaudatus $X_{Ni}X_{Ch}$ × ♂ nigrocaudatus $X_{Ni}Y_{Ir}$

F₂ (2:1:1)

♀ nigrocaudatus $X_{Ni}X_{Ni}$ — ♂ nigrocaudatus $X_{Ni}Y_{Ir}$

♀ nigrocaudatus $X_{Ni}X_{Ch}$ × ♂ iridescent $X_{Ch}Y_{Ir}$

F₃ (1:1:1:1)

♀ nigrocaudatus $X_{Ni}X_{Ch}$ — ♂ nigrocaudatus $X_{Ni}Y_{Ir}$

♀ wild $X_{Ch}X_{Ch}$ — ♂ iridescent $X_{Ch}Y_{Ir}$

The crossing of guppies with the character nigrocaudatus (Tuxedo) and the character iridescence is an example of epistatic inheritance. The character nigrocaudatus (X_{Ni} X_{Ni}), resulting in the black coloring of the caudal root, is linked to the **X**-chromosome. This means it can occur in male and female alike. The character iridescence ($X_{Ch}Y_{Ir}$) is bound to the **Y**-chromosome, the male sex chromosome. Nigrocaudatus is "stronger" than iridescence, which explains why the males of the first generation—although containing the factor for iridescence in their **Y**-chromosome—look like pure nigrocaudatus males. Only later, in the second and third generations (F₂ and F₃), we again observe males that show the iridescent coloring. The factor nigrocaudatus is absent in their **X**-chromosome because the mother was a heterozygous form, and so the factor "iridescence" is able to express itself once more.

Opposite:

Sex-linked inheritance. The trait iridescence occurs only in the male guppy. It expresses itself in the form of a red patch at the base of the caudal fin. The hereditary factor for this characteristic is located on the **Y**-chromosome. Only the sons, never the daughters, show this trait and carry the hereditary factor for it.

oration as the Tuxedo on the peduncle. With the female it is best to choose a specimen with a large body, a faint flame pattern on the caudal fin from top to bottom, and a large upper portion on the fin.

When you cannot get hold of suitable Mosaic specimens for breeding, take a female Grass, King Cobra or other established variety on hand and mate it with a Mosaic male. F_1 is all crossbreeds; but then breed F_2 and F_3 from within the litter and select the Mosaics. This will not be a problem with males whose external appearance makes them easy to recognize. With females, however, it is important to use care in selecting specimens that exhibit true Mosaic characteristics. Through repeated inbreeding the fish will then approach the target type.

King Cobra Family

In the King Cobra variety there are numerous variations: King Cobra, Mosaic Cobra, Lace Cobra, etc. When you look at caudal fin design, too, there are Grass, Leopard, Mosaic, Lace, etc. Here, I will speak about points of commonality to watch out for between Cobra strains and the generic types.

For the Cobra male, it is important that it have a fine Cobra pattern over its entire body (from the tip of the head to the end of the caudal peduncle). It is preferable not to use a specimen with pink or red coloration at the peduncle, with the cobra design not clearly shown on this area, or where the length (in the case of fish, the side view) has lines on it or, to use laymen's terms, where the length has a band or zebra pattern. The Cobra pattern is a dominant trait, but if you do not carefully select your specimens before breeding, you will be vexed by reddish caudal markings and a band design that will surely appear and give you trouble.

For the King Cobra female, the best specimen is transparent with a rounded tail. But most females have a pointed upper caudal edge or they have ink blots or spots on their fins. You have to select the best from among these, looking for a true King Cobra female to pair up with the male. With King Cobras these days, you have to begin by getting litters from several types of females of the same litter and then gleaning from those the ones that would be the most genuine specimen for the male. You establish the strain by repeated inbreeding of F_1, F_2, and F_3; then you break down the genealogy into the main and subordinate lineages. Next, you cross the respective lines and breed them. In this way, the genealogy is maintained.

The Mosaic Cobra female cannot be distinguished from the Mosaic female at just a glance because the former has the same caudal fin, coloration, design, and shape as the Mosaic. In maintaining the Mosaic Cobra, it is good not to just mate within the same line but also occasionally to mate a Mosaic Cobra male with a Mosaic female.

The Lace-type female is plain with a rounded tail. You can maintain this strain even if you mate the female with other Cobra-types, if you are careful to select and mate the plain-colored, round-tailed specimens.

Grass

If we broadly subdivide the Grass variety, we have the Grass Grass, in which the Grass design on the caudal fin is very delicate and fine compared to the Mosaic, and the Glass Grass, in which a spot-like design appears against a background transparent like glass. Recently, Red Grass has also been produced by crossbreeding with a Red Mosaic;

Regardless of how plain the guppies you start with, improvement will occur if they are provided with the proper conditions and the progeny are culled selectively over the course of time.

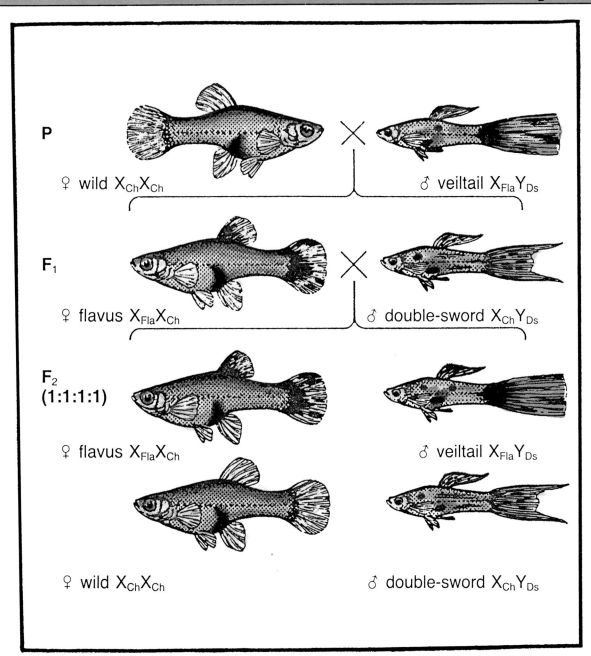

Crossing of a wild-type female guppy with a male veiltail. The first generation (F₁) comprises females with yellow tail fins and double-sword males. In the second generation (F₂), then, we get females with yellow tail fins, wild-type females, veiltail males, and double-sword males.

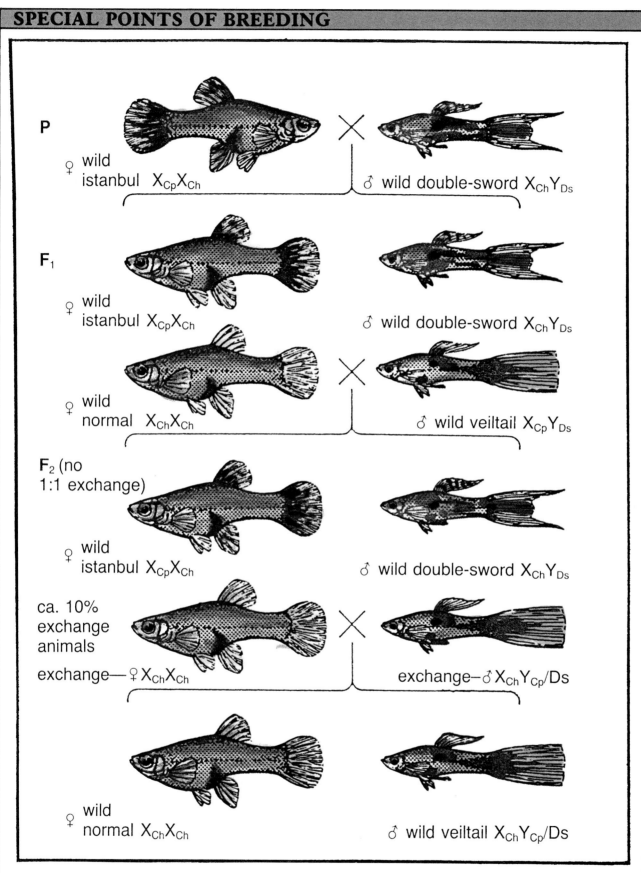

P ♀ wild istanbul $X_{Cp}X_{Ch}$ × ♂ wild double-sword $X_{Ch}Y_{Ds}$

F₁ ♀ wild istanbul $X_{Cp}X_{Ch}$ ♂ wild double-sword $X_{Ch}Y_{Ds}$

♀ wild normal $X_{Ch}X_{Ch}$ × ♂ wild veiltail $X_{Cp}Y_{Ds}$

F₂ (no 1:1 exchange) ♀ wild istanbul $X_{Cp}X_{Ch}$ ♂ wild double-sword $X_{Ch}Y_{Ds}$

ca. 10% exchange animals

exchange— ♀ $X_{Ch}X_{Ch}$ × exchange–♂ $X_{Ch}Y_{Cp}/Ds$

♀ wild normal $X_{Ch}X_{Ch}$ ♂ wild veiltail $X_{Ch}Y_{Cp}/Ds$

The combination of a hereditary factor for coloring **(Cp)** with a hereditary factor for the extension of the caudal fin rays **(Ds)** results in veiltail guppies: the color gene causes the double sword tail fin to fill up with membrane.

Occasionally an exchange of genes occurs between homologous chromosomes ("crossing-over"). In our example the F₂ generation includes about 10% of "exchange guppies." This exchange between the factor **Cp** from the **X**-chromosome and the factor **Ds** from the **Y**-chromosome leads to a new stable strain with a veiltail in the male guppy.

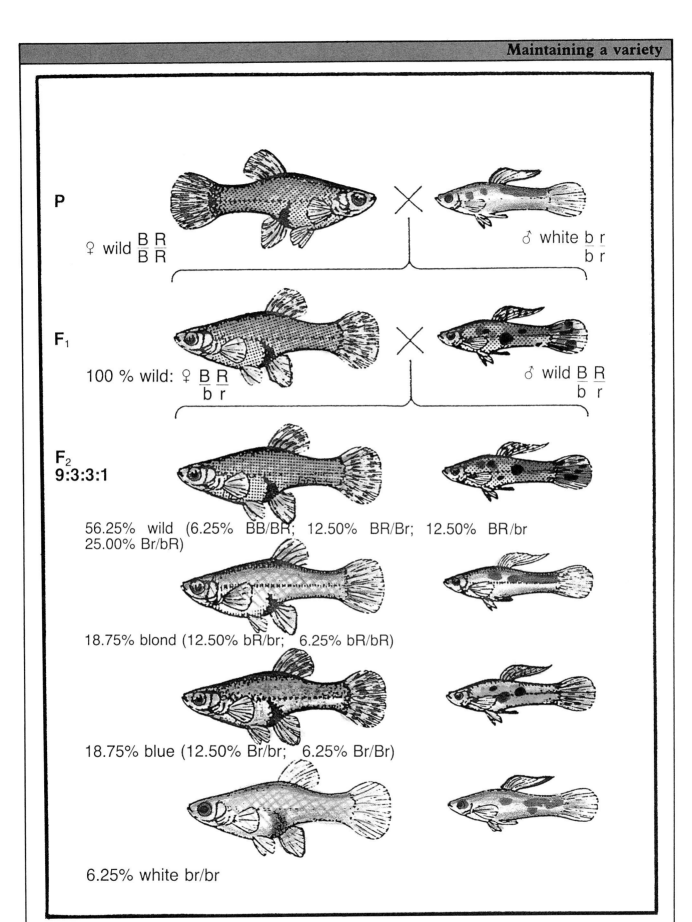

P

♀ wild $\frac{B}{B}\frac{R}{R}$ ✕   ♂ white $\frac{b}{b}\frac{r}{r}$

F₁

100 % wild: ♀ $\frac{B}{b}\frac{R}{r}$ ✕   ♂ wild $\frac{B}{b}\frac{R}{r}$

F₂
9:3:3:1

56.25% wild (6.25% BB/BR; 12.50% BR/Br; 12.50% BR/br 25.00% Br/bR)

18.75% blond (12.50% bR/br; 6.25% bR/bR)

18.75% blue (12.50% Br/br; 6.25% Br/Br)

6.25% white br/br

If guppies with two (or more) pairs of characters are crossed, the two characteristics are transmitted independently of each other, provided the genes concerned are located on different, non-homologous chromosomes. Our diagram shows the crossing of a white guppy male with a normal wild-colored female. The guppies of the first daughter generation (F₁) are all wild-colored. In the second daughter generation (F₂) the traits segregate. We get wild-type, blond, blue, and white guppies. Only the white guppies are always homozygous.

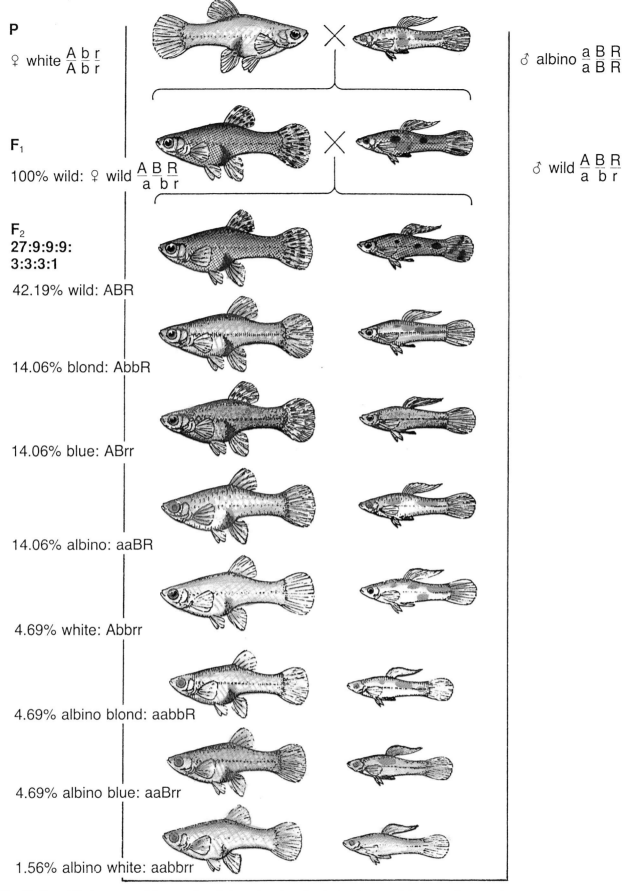

P

♀ white $\dfrac{A}{A}\dfrac{b}{b}\dfrac{r}{r}$

♂ albino $\dfrac{a}{a}\dfrac{B}{B}\dfrac{R}{R}$

F₁

100% wild: ♀ wild $\dfrac{A}{a}\dfrac{B}{b}\dfrac{R}{r}$

♂ wild $\dfrac{A}{a}\dfrac{B}{b}\dfrac{R}{r}$

F₂
27:9:9:9:
3:3:3:1

42.19% wild: ABR

14.06% blond: AbbR

14.06% blue: ABrr

14.06% albino: aaBR

4.69% white: Abbrr

4.69% albino blond: aabbR

4.69% albino blue: aaBrr

1.56% albino white: aabbrr

The likelihood that a cross of three pairs of characters is going to produce a triple-recessive type is a mere 1/64 (1.56%) in the F₂ generation. In our example, a white guppy female was crossed with an albino male. The first daughter generation was wild-colored throughout. In the second daughter generation eight different types were segregated out, the rarest one of these being the albino-white, which contains two each of the three recessive genes **a, b, r** (homozygous).

Yellow Grass has emerged from crossing with a Leopard; and Blue Grass, thought to be the product of mating with a Neon Tuxedo, has been produced. Each of the first two Grass strains has its respective red and blue types. Accordingly, it is critical that you know the type of crossbreeding that produced your seed specimens in order for you to maintain the lineage properly.

For the Grass male, it is best to select one whose caudal is not black and whose design extends uniformly across the fin, not breaking down in the middle. A round-tailed plain female is best, but when this variety is established, many females will have inky marks or spots on the caudal fin.

Red Grass are early developers so be careful to choose as your seed a specimen that is fully grown. If you breed carefully selected seed fish, this lineage is relatively easy to maintain because it is quite stable. Of course, it goes without saying that even though the line is highly established, the major premise for successful selective breeding continues to be that appropriate quality males and females be selected as seeds.

Yellow Grass is a new strain, so it is not yet clearly established. It is classified as Grass and Leopard, so you can crossbreed either strain in order to support the lineage.

Blue Grass is a new type of Grass. In choosing the male, keep those specimens that have spotted caudals on a pale blue background and get rid of others in the litter. Selecting the female is very difficult. It seems as though females having rounded caudals with pale ink marks on the upper portion bear good litters, but this is not certain.

Leopard

In supporting the Leopard line it is common to use a King Cobra female. The Cobra influence then remains well into the future, so it is necessary to use rigor in the selection process. One other interesting method is to crossbreed with Yellow Grass, keeping the babies that most resemble the Leopard and then reverse breeding them. When you select your specimens remove those with red coloration on the caudal fin as they do not conform with the Leopard image. The Leopard female is simple and round-tailed.

The contemporary Leopard in Japan has come to differ considerably from the Leopard imported from Germany and America. In actuality it is im-possible to duplicate exactly the color and design of the Leopards that were first introduced into Japan. Therefore, we had to produce a new Leopard, using the real-life leopard image as the central image for breeding. If you do not do this, then it will become impossible to differentiate the Leopard from the Yellow Grass.

Tuxedo

The peak of breeding achievement in the Tuxedo variety is the German Yellow Tuxedo, but these specimens often produce deformed or abnormally small offspring. As a result, there are few fish suitable for seeds, making it quite difficult to support the genealogy. In addition to this complication, litters are small and many babies do not survive to maturity. If, regarding this as an adverse consequence of close inbreeding, you then crossbreed with another variety, things usually do not go well. You may get F_1 but not be able to proceed from there, or you will have difficulty recreating the peculiar silken hues of the caudal fin.

To the greatest extent possible, when conducting direct line breeding select a female that does not have red coloration or blotches on its caudal. Then interbreed it with a male of strong physical constitution. In crossbreeding with other varieties, the Neon Tuxedo is often used, but you do not want markings to show up on the babies' caudal fins so it is best to choose a female with a patternless tail.

The Mosaic Tuxedo is maintained in parallel with the regular Mosaic line; occasionally the two are crossed to protect from a scattered Mosaic design. Be careful here because if you select as your seed fish a specimen whose caudal is too dark a red, the offspring will be black.

With other types like the Neon Tuxedo and the Red Tail Tuxedo, the basic technique for supporting the lineage is the same as for other strains. However, since the caudal turns black with excessive breeding within the same genealogy, it is beneficial to regularly crossbreed with a separate lineage or another variety.

Sword Tail

Supporting the Bottom Sword and Double Sword strains is comparatively easy. If you mate a round-tailed, plain-colored female with a male that has a large dorsal fin and a caudal fin that clearly exhibits the characteristics of the given strain, then

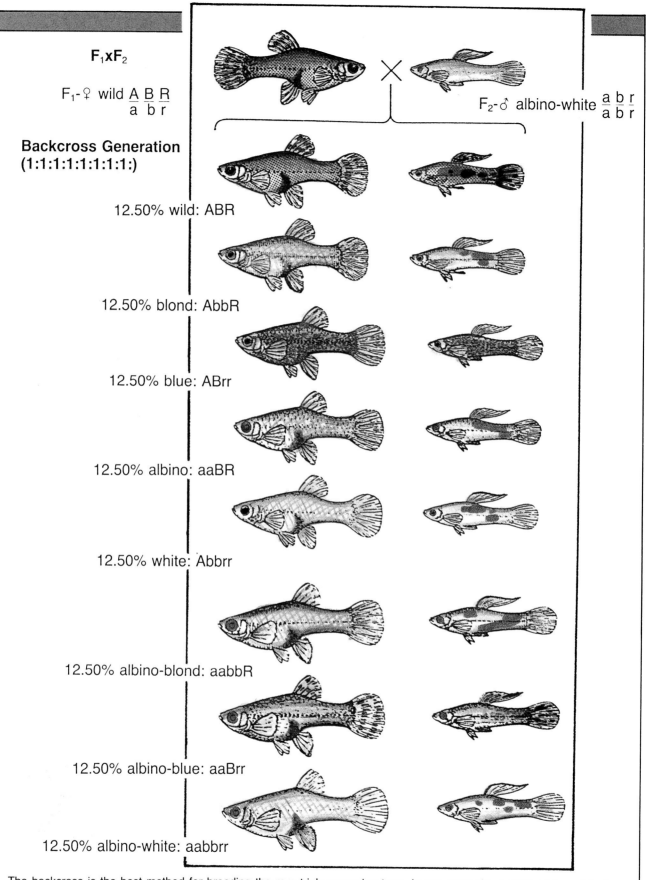

F₁xF₂

F₁- ♀ wild $\frac{A}{a} \frac{B}{b} \frac{R}{r}$

F₂- ♂ albino-white $\frac{a}{a} \frac{b}{b} \frac{r}{r}$

Backcross Generation
(1:1:1:1:1:1:1:1:)

12.50% wild: ABR

12.50% blond: AbbR

12.50% blue: ABrr

12.50% albino: aaBR

12.50% white: Abbrr

12.50% albino-blond: aabbR

12.50% albino-blue: aaBrr

12.50% albino-white: aabbrr

The backcross is the best method for breeding the rare triple-recessive type. In our example, a male albino-white from the F₂ generation is crossed with a wild-type female from the F₁ generation. This increases the chance of getting homozygous albino-white guppies to 12.5%.

you can maintain it over a rather long time simply by direct line breeding. This is a variety that can be enjoyed with just one aquarium as long as you conscientiously select and weed out poor specimens.

A Tiger Tuxedo. The longfin type is very difficult to produce.

This is a Bottom Swordtail guppy, the foundation of selective breeding in the Tiger strain.

A Top Sword produced by mating a Cobra of the Tiger strain with a Bottom Sword.

A young Redtail Tuxedo of the Tiger strain. The plants in the background are almost a necessity with guppies.

A Tiger Bottom Sword female. The black-bordered scales are lovely.

This Golden-type Mosaic, with a perfect Delta tail, is
very difficult to produce.

This fish is the same strain as above. In order to keep
this strain pure, you should selectively breed only the
best males with the best females.

Golden Type

Each basic variety has its Golden type. In general, the Golden type is weaker than the regular strain.

Maintaining the Golden line is not very difficult. It is preferable not to mate only Golden pairs but to crossbreed regularly with ordinary strains.

Left and right above: Japanese-bred Golden Cobra guppies. The lace design on the caudal fin is very attractive, but the caudal tears easily in this variety.

A cross between a Red Tail Tuxedo and a Flamingo produced this male.

Golden Grass male with delicately patterned tail.

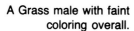

A Grass male with faint coloring overall.

A Tiger Cobra with an interesting tail fin pattern and coloration. The spots on its back are attractive.

A spectacular large tail on a Tiger Red Tail Tuxedo.

A Tiger Red Tail Tuxedo. This is an energetic specimen with a large dorsal fin.

A Grass tail on a Tiger body makes a very photogenic fish.

A rare Black Tuxedo Tiger.

This Golden was produced by crossing a Golden
Mosaic with a Cobra. The tail fin splits easily.

A Longfin Golden Mosaic female. The transparent tail
is gorgeous.

A beautiful Golden Grass with a metallic shine.

A Longfin Golden which is very difficult to produce.

Albino Type

As with the Golden, Albinos exist in each of the basic guppy varieties, but they are weaker still.

If you continuously mate only Albino pairs, weakness, deformity, female infertility, and similar negative effects will manifest themselves. Roughly three generations is the limit for breeding within a direct line. Then before quality deteriorates, interbreed with the regular variety. The F_1 born of a regular strain and an Albino are all of the regular variety; approximately twenty-five percent of F_2 will be Albino.

Tiger

The unique characteristics of the Tiger, its sep-ia-colored body and black-edged scales, are passed on genetically in the same way as albinism. As such, the abnormalities associated with close inbreeding appear comparatively early, so you have to crossbreed with regular varieties to maintain the Tiger lineage.

To illustrate with a concrete example, the F_1 born of a regular Bottom Sword male and a Tiger Bottom Sword female will all be ordinary Bottom Swords. If you mate within F_1, F_2 should be twenty-five percent Tiger Bottom Sword and the rest are regular Bottom Swords. When you breed within F_2 to get F_3, some litters have ordinary Bottom Swords and possibly a few Tiger Bottom Swords.

BREEDING TIGER BOTTOM SWORDS

A Tiger Bottom Sword female (tt) is crossed with a regular Bottom Sword male (RR). All of the males produced look like the father, a regular Bottom Sword, but they carry the recessive Tiger gene, t.

It takes two generations to produce Tiger Bottom Swords. The second step is on the facing page.

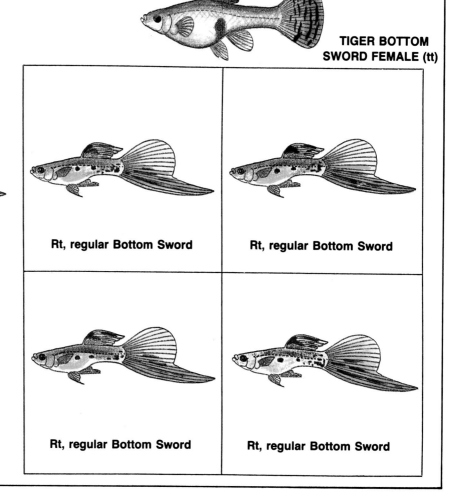

TIGER BOTTOM SWORD FEMALE (tt)

REGULAR BOTTOM SWORD, MALE (RR)

Rt, regular Bottom Sword	Rt, regular Bottom Sword
Rt, regular Bottom Sword	Rt, regular Bottom Sword

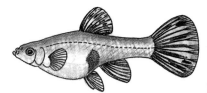

FEMALE Rt

MALE Rt

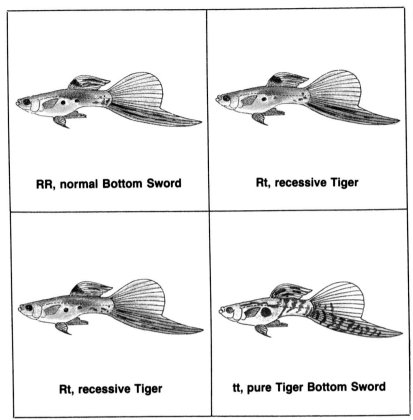

RR, normal Bottom Sword	**Rt, recessive Tiger**
Rt, recessive Tiger	**tt, pure Tiger Bottom Sword**

BREEDING TIGER BOTTOM SWORDS, SECOND GENERATION
By breeding an Rt female produced in the first generation with one of her brothers of Rt composition, you will get 25% Tiger Bottom Swords, 25% normal Bottom Swords, and 50% recessive Tiger Bottom Swords which look like normal Bottom Swords.

Maintaining the Albino Lineage

It is often said that maintaining the Albino strain is difficult, but that is not necessarily so. In supporting the albino line there are several points to remember, so I would like to discuss them in concrete terms.

First, the Albino is afflicted by a pigment deficiency disease, so it necessary to be aware of this obstacle. Compared with regular varieties, the Albino is feeble and has weak reproductive capabilities. Thus, when you mate Albino pairs after two or three generations, either you cannot get a litter or even if you can, many specimens will be deformed or dwarfed and in the end the lines die out. In other words, if you mate deformed fish in order to establish a genealogy, it is impossible to get non-deformed offspring. Therefore, you always have to crossbreed with healthy specimens of regular varieties and support the Albino line by remaking it each generation.

When you purchase Albino specimens, you want to buy two or three pairs if your budget allows, because the strain has such weak reproductive capacity. (Simply put, many cannot produce a litter.) Then, with young pairs about three or four months old, select a male that actively chases the females and a female with a glamorous body that is sufficiently extended in the abdomen. On the female, you also want to be able to see orange eggs if you look carefully at the lower abdominal region. Among Albino females some specimens have flat abdomens or veins and intestines visible in the

If you look closely at the anal area of this female, you can almost see the eyes of the fry about to be born. Photo by Andre Roth.

lower stomach. These females often do not produce young, so exercise caution in making your selections. If you look closely at a heavily pregnant female's lower abdomen, you will see protruding eyes in the eggs. You will certainly get offspring from this sort of female.

Many Albino parents will eat their young. This may be because they have poor visual ability and/or because newly born Albino babies are mistaken for food. If a litter is born in a regular tank without you noticing it, almost all babies will be eaten. Since it is hard to detect a female's first pregnancy, it is best to move her to a spawning box a bit early.

A spawning aquarium with lots of lush water plants is not appropriate for Albinos; a simple spawning box is better. When the female drops her litter, mark the date on your calendar. If she's healthy, the next litter will be born in about thirty days. Watch and move her just before that date.

If things go smoothly like this and you get a lit-ter early on from the seed fish you purchased, there are no problems with the fish. On the other hand, if there are no signs of pregnancy one month after purchase, this means that the male or female (or, in the worst case, both) are infertile.

As a countermeasure I would like to discuss a technique often used to support Albino varieties.

Mate an Albino female with a male of a regular strain. All of the F_1 will show regular characteristics. The F_1 appear regular but they carry the Albino gene. (However, in cases where the male looks regular but carries an Albino gene, a small number of Albinos may be born in F_1.) If you mate the regular offspring of the F_1 born from a regular male and an Albino female, about fifty percent of F_2 will manifest albino traits. If you mate the Albinos from F_2, then all of F_3 will show albinism. Then, when you move to F_4, F_5, and succeeding generations you cannot maintain the line because deformities, dwarfism, and feebleness begin to appear. Before this happens, breed the Albinos with regular specimens as you did earlier to get F₁. By repeating this entire process you can preserve the Albino genealogy.

Regarding the regular strain males used in the crossbreeding, it is best to use specimens of basically the same genealogy as the Albino: if the Albino is an Albino Grass, use a Grass male; if it is an Albino King Cobra, use a King Cobra male,

and so on. If you mate with a different strain, you will get regular offspring displaying dominant traits in F₁, but it is not certain that you will get the Albinos you are aiming for in F₂. In particular, if you mate with a King Cobra even once, its influence is in evidence over many generations. Thus, I strongly recommend that you use a regular specimen of the same type.

THE BEST WAY TO PRODUCE GOOD ALBINOS IS WITH A TWO STEP BREEDING PROGRAM.
The first step is to cross a gray (wild type) male, GG, with an albino female, aa. Albinos are always pure recessive.

ALBINO FEMALE, aa

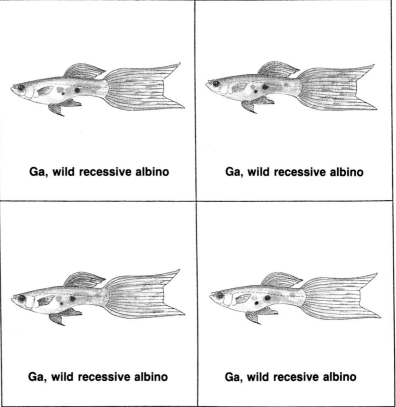

GRAY MALE GG

Ga, wild recessive albino

Ga, wild recessive albino

Ga, wild recessive albino

Ga, wild recesive albino

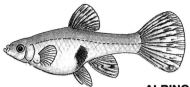

ALBINO FEMALE, aa

**WILD-TYPE
MALE WITH
RECESSIVE
ALBINISM
Ga**

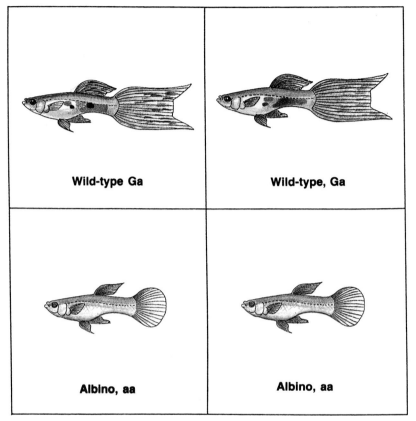

Wild-type Ga	Wild-type, Ga
Albino, aa	Albino, aa

**THE FINAL PRODUCTION OF ALBINOS IS TO CROSS A Ga, WILD-TYPE RECESSIVE MALE
PRODUCED IN THE FIRST GENERATION (See previous page) WITH AN ALBINO MOTHER.
With this type of cross you can expect 50% albino and 50% recessive wild-type as shown above.**

Long Fin

To broadly divide the Long Fin type, there is the Long Fin (Swallow) type in which each fin extends irregularly and the Ribbon type in which one fin (especially the anal fin) is elongated. The genetics of these two types are different. First, the Long Fin type can be maintained through F_1 and F_2 by mating with the regular males of the same litter. If, at that time, you use a Long Fin female, you will get lots of Long Fin babies. However, decline in quality also accelerates with such a technique. Stronger offspring will be produced if you use a female that looks normal but carries the Long Fin gene.

Conversely, when a Ribbon type female is mated with a regular male, Ribbon offspring definitely appear. In other words, maintaining this variety is easy because even if you do not always breed within the same litter, the results will be successful as long as you use a virgin Long Fin female.

Inheritance of veiled fins in the Berlin guppy after the mating of a veil fin guppy female with a normal-finned guppy male from the same strain (segregation 1:1).

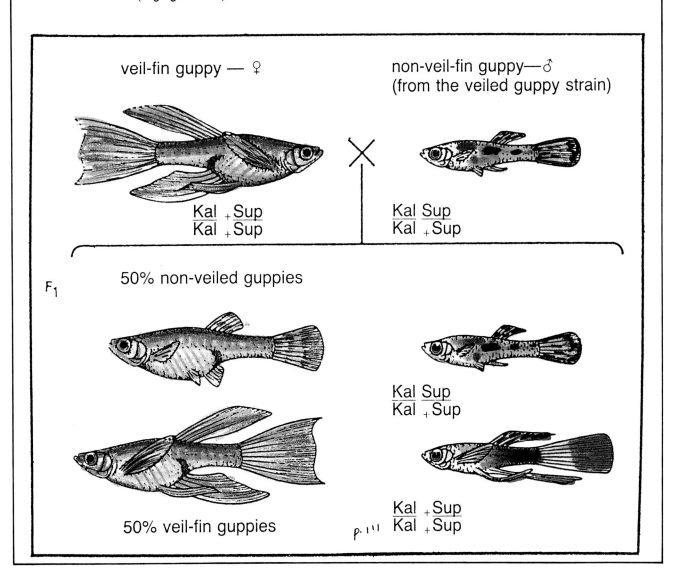

veil-fin guppy — ♀

non-veil-fin guppy—♂
(from the veiled guppy strain)

$\dfrac{Kal_{+}Sup}{Kal_{+}Sup}$

$\dfrac{Kal\ Sup}{Kal_{+}Sup}$

F_1

50% non-veiled guppies

$\dfrac{Kal\ Sup}{Kal_{+}Sup}$

50% veil-fin guppies

$\dfrac{Kal_{+}Sup}{Kal_{+}Sup}$

123

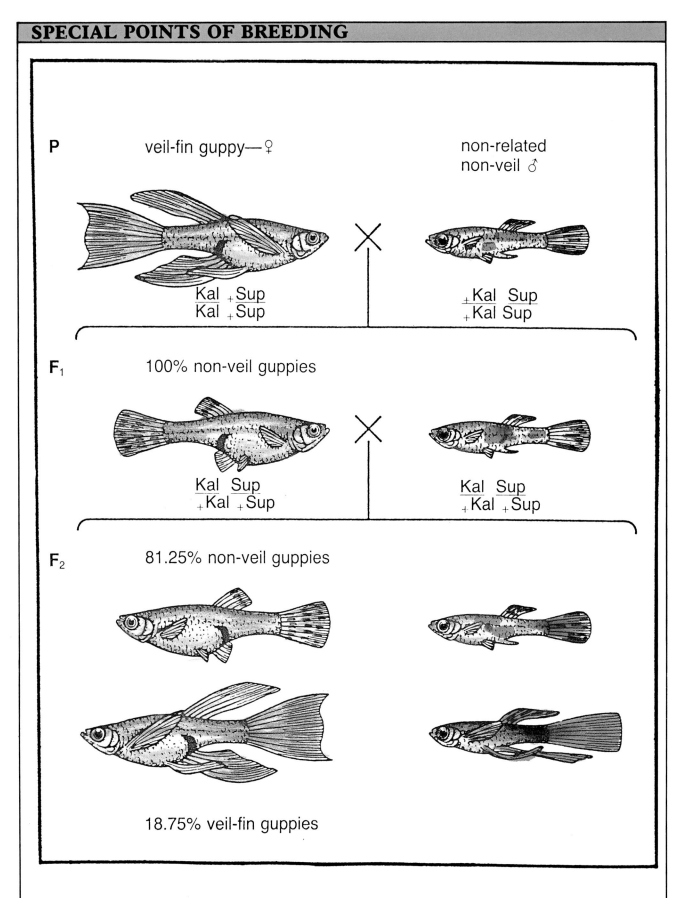

P   veil-fin guppy—♀   non-related
                                  non-veil ♂

$$\frac{Kal}{Kal} {}_{+}\frac{Sup}{{}_{+}Sup}$$ $${}_{+}\frac{Kal}{{}_{+}Kal}\frac{Sup}{Sup}$$

F₁   100% non-veil guppies

$$\frac{Kal}{{}_{+}Kal}\frac{Sup}{{}_{+}Sup}$$ $$\frac{Kal}{{}_{+}Kal}\frac{Sup}{{}_{+}Sup}$$

F₂   81.25% non-veil guppies

18.75% veil-fin guppies

Inheritance of veiled fins in the Berlin guppy after the mating of a veiled guppy female with a non-related normal-finned male (F₂ segregation 13:3).

Introducing Foreign-Produced Guppy Specimens

Recently the volume and improved quality of imported guppies have forced enthusiasts to take notice. You find lots of marvelous imported guppies with many variations in fin and body color and design, especially in the King Cobra and Tuxedo varieties. That such wonderful guppies can be shipped every week gives evidence of the high level techniques being used.

During the earlier guppy boom, many people were dissatisfied with imported guppies; some people blamed problems with imported specimens for the end to the boom. However, if you understand the essentials of good guppy care and breeding, you cannot distinguish magnificent guppies by country of origin. On the other hand, you cannot

The Japanese editon of this book featured this magnificent fish on its back cover. It is a very short-bodied, fully finned guppy.

The Germans refer to this type of fish as Flamingo. Photo by Burkhard Kahl.

Three-quarter black Tuxedo. Photo
by Dr. Herbert R. Axelrod.

get around problems with reproductive ability, degree of reliability, and differing conditions of care, so place of origin should not be completely ignored.

As when using young domestic guppies for selective breeding, when you use imported guppies the key point is to make sure that specimens are to some degree established. If you use fish with low reliability as your seeds, F_1 might be spectacular but things will probably not go well from F_2 on. Be aware that in the process of producing a new type of guppy, the "strain" is considered only partly developed until some degree of reliability is achieved.

Next, I would like to discuss practical steps for working with imported guppies.

First, create an image of the type of fish you would like to produce. What you actually use as a base for selective breeding is one of your own female specimens. Using a female you already have in your possession for selective breeding is the best road to success. Then, prepare three pairs. Each

Very rare German Yellow. Photo by
Dr. Herbert R. Axelrod.

pair should include a domestic female whose swollen stomach and blackened lower abdomen make her appear to be ready to give birth, and an imported male that has a well-balanced body that seems to be a larger version of a domestic guppy— one that actively pursues female specimens and conforms to your image of what you want to create.

With foreign produced guppies, it is necessary to adjust the water temperature and remove salt from the water just before mating. Prepare a small ten to twenty-gallon aquarium and initially set the temperature at 27 to 28 degrees centigrade. Put three spoonfuls of salt and a small amount of methylene blue to help prevent disease. After two days change the water; for ten days to two weeks use regular neutralized tap water kept at 22 to 24 degrees centigrade.

Put the female of the foreign pair in a separate tank and let her give birth as usual. In raising these baby fish, watch their condition for about three months (by which time the special characteristics of their strain will appear). Then systematically mate those that seem usable for selective breeding and dispose of the others.

The three males should be put in a tank and mated with your own females that were prepared earlier. If all goes well, the litters will be born in about thirty days. After that, raise the babies the same as usual: as they grow, separate the males from the females and keep several of each for producing the next generation. Keep on selecting and weeding out until you get the kind of fish you are aiming for.

The Joy of Producing a New Variety

The interesting aspect of breeding guppies lies in creating your own fish. The definition of "your own fish" includes those specimens produced when you buy or otherwise come into possession of fish, use them as seeds to produce F_1, and then mate within F_1 to get F_2. It also includes instances in which you mate a female you already have with a male you newly acquire. Fish that you bought and raised or the F_1 produced from these are not ordinarily considered fish that you have created. What is more, in the world of guppies it is frowned upon to exhibit such guppies in contests.

Because selective breeding is conducted with your own image of coloration, fin shape, and de-

The male's anal fin becomes modified into a sex organ called a 'gonopodium'.

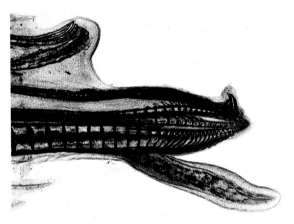

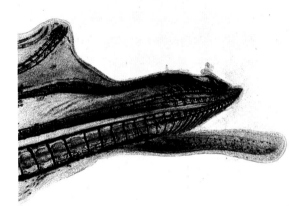

A guppy's gonopodium. The photo on the right is a Japanese guppy; the one on the left is an imported one.

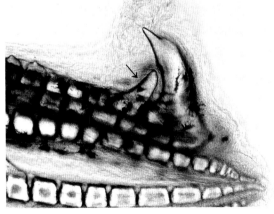

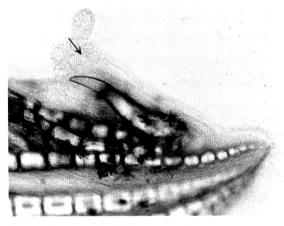

A similar enlargement of an imported guppy's gonopodium. Notice the locking mechanism (arrow). This may indicate a difference between Japanese guppies and imported ones.

The hook on the tip of this gonopodium (arrow) is a holdfast organ which the male uses to penetrate the female and hold her momentarily as his sperm is extruded.

These beautiful Flamingo guppies were produced in Czechoslovakia. Photo by Ruda Zukal.

These German guppies were bred for the single characteristic of tail enhancement. Photo by Burkhard Kahl.

sign in mind, you feel an indescribable satisfaction when that image is actually realized. As such, guppy breeding can be said to be the highest level of hobby.

Selective breeding begins with establishing a variety through systematic mating. The best method for producing your target type is to mate between different established strains then repeat the selecting and weeding out processes. Mating hybrids does no more than increase the number of hybrids. Even if on rare occasions a spectacular F_1 is born from crossing two hybrids, most will only be so-called "one-generation mixed breeds."

When your objective is selective breeding of guppies, reliability is naturally important; but if your interest is out-of-the-ordinary specimens, you can enjoy crossing a variety of types without worrying about the rigorous weeding out process necessary for systematic breeding. Actually, the current tendency has been for increasing numbers of people to enjoy one-generation guppy types.

Crossing specimens of different established varieties, called outbreeding, is the basic technique of selective breeding.

An F_1 born of outbreeding becomes a hybrid, sharing qualities of both parents. If you mate within F_1, the resulting F_2 can be broken down into those similar to the F_1 type and those with the qualities of one of the original parents. If you systematically breed the respective F_2 types, selecting and weeding out poor specimens, the possibility of producing a new strain develops. After that, if you can maintain a particular characteristic, those guppies can become a new variety. However, actual guppy varieties are not perfectly established so it is definitely a difficult job. But if you start breeding with the goal of raising reliability as high as possible and you keep at it patiently, you will surely be able to produce the type of guppies you wish to produce.

It sometimes happens with guppies that there are specimens with mutations or those that are quite unlike the parents. These are usually one-generation mixed breeds, but if you put them to use, you can create a completely new type.

There are many laws of genetics, but with guppies the results do not necessarily turn out as the rules would suggest. Yet, to conduct genetic research on the basis of actual practical experience is very useful for selective breeding. Let me point

out several examples from my recent research.

These days you do not see many domestic Red Tails, so I tried to breed some. There are two methods to do this: One is to breed an Albino Red Tail with another variety, get regular Red Tails in F_1 and establish them; the other is to get F_1 by mating Flamingo with another variety. I opted for the latter approach.

First, I mated a Flamingo female with a Red Tail Tuxedo male. The F_1 males turned out to be Red Tails and the females were Red Tail Tuxedos. Mating within the litter, four types of F_2 males emerged: Red Tail, Red Tail Tuxedo, Flamingo, and Golden Red Tail Tuxedo. Females of corresponding types were also born. From these F_2 types I took the Red Tail and Golden Red Tail Tuxedo as object types. I intend to establish them by repeated selection and weeding out.

Secondly, several years ago, a Bottom Sword Tiger reappeared on the market, though it was slightly different from the Tiger type of old. It was a wild, marvelous variety, but it was very difficult to maintain because large numbers of specimens just died of unknown causes.

The male is brown with black-edged scales and some red or orange hues on the body, but it is rather dull. The female is cute, having the same basic coloration as the male, but no color on the body.

Among Bottom Swords of the Grass variety, there is a strain called Lace Bottom that has a design on the peduncle that resembles the design on a bowl for Chinese noodles, has a beautiful metallic body, and also is highly established. All females are plain and round-finned.

I set out to produce a Tiger Lace Bottom Sword that combined the pattern and strong body characteristics of the Lace Bottom with the coloration of the Tiger Bottom Sword.

First I mated a Tiger Bottom Sword female with a Lace Bottom male. F_1 males were all Lace Bottoms. The females were all plain, with basic gray coloration and rounded fins. I then mated within F_1 and in F_2. I got Lace Bottoms, Tiger Bottoms, Tiger Bottom Swords, and my target type, Tiger Lace Bottom Swords. After that, I mated and crossed the various types to move closer to perfecting the Tiger Lace Bottom.

During this process, when I crossed Lace Bottom males and females of the same litter, some

This Japanese Flamingo has a nice Delta tail. The red on the caudal area could be brighter.

An unusual Japanese Red Tail. The large spread of the tail is magnificent.

broods were only Lace Bottom and some were only Tiger type. From these results, one understands that Tiger type guppy characteristics are genetically transmitted in the same manner as Albinos: if you cross a Tiger with a regular strain specimen, you get regular babies in F_1 and Tigers appear in F_2.

From this example, you can understand the method by which to create variations of the Tiger.

Female Fantails are glamorous with their large tails
and close resemblance to Mosaics.

Another German strain sports a metallic body shine
extending even into the large dorsal fin.

The old-fashioned Fantail is a new type developed from German imports.

A fish of separate lineage imported from Germany. This Fantail has a Flame design.

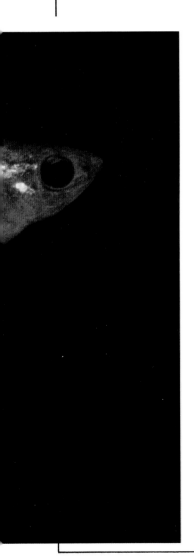

The third example involves the Mosaic Cobra, a hybrid born from selectively breeding the King Cobra; it is a beautiful strain with a red mosaic pattern against yellow and black on the caudal fin and a Cobra design on the body against metallic green coloring.

In order to develop the typical mosaic pattern on the caudal fin, I crossed a Red Mosaic female with a male King Cobra that had yellow and black caudal. The F_1 males exhibited a combination of the parents' qualities—all had Cobra bodies and Mosaic tails. The females all had the same typical Mosaic characteristics as the mother: a caudal fin that widens at the top and is a faint blue with a flame-like pattern. If you saw only the females in the brood you probably could not distinguish them from Mosaic females.

Five different types of males were seen in F_2: King Cobra, Red Mosaic, Mosaic Cobra, Golden Cobra with Mosaic caudal fins, and Golden Cobra with Lace caudals. The fact that Golden types emerged can be thought of as an expression of the same influence causing Red Mosaics previously to bear Golden types.

The implication seems to be that a pattern exists suggesting that Goldens are often born of Red Tails. The F_2 females included females that had Mosaic caudals just as in F_1 and King Cobra females.

From the F_2, I mated Mosaic Cobra males and females, mated F_3 and F_4 within their litters, and parallel to this also mated them with Mosaics. At present, I am maintaining two lineages, a principal one and a subsidiary one.

CROSSING A KING COBRA MALE WITH A RED MOSAIC FEMALE
This cross produces Red Mosaic females and Red Mosaic Cobra males.

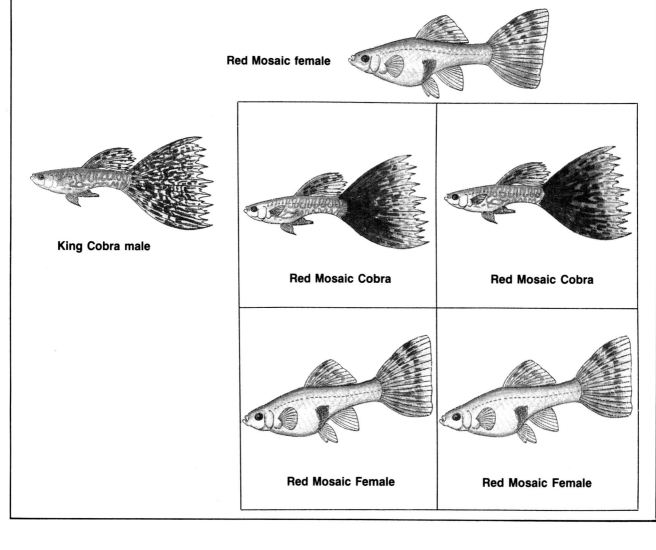

Red Mosaic female

King Cobra male

Red Mosaic Cobra

Red Mosaic Cobra

Red Mosaic Female

Red Mosaic Female

Both the Mosaic and the Lace Golden Cobras that turned up in F$_2$ were quite feeble and though they produced some young, they died before becoming fully grown.

Another example comes from within the Cobra variety; the Lace Cobra is a lovely strain with a finely patterned caudal fin that reminds me of lace curtains. It is one of my favorites.

If you mate a King Cobra male with a Bottom Sword female, then you get Lace Cobras in F$_1$. Select colorless, round-tailed females and repeat the breeding of F$_2$ and F$_3$ and the line will become completely established.

This may be superfluous, but when I crossed a King Cobra male with a Tiger Bottom Sword female, I got Top Sword Lace Cobras in F$_1$, but they were weak and unable to produce young fish.

The final example deals with a Fantail. Recently, the old fashioned Fan Tail, was introduced into Japan. In addition to breeding within a litter I also crossed it with several other varieties. This guppy is extremely robust. I was pleased to be able to get an F$_1$ from Albino Mosaics and Albino Tuxedos, which I previously had not been able to fertilize.

The F$_1$ obtained from crossing an old fashioned Fan Tail male with an Albino Red Tail female included Red Tails and Bottom Swords. Both types have wonderful coloration, with vivid caudal fin hues and shiny bodies. I have high hopes for F$_2$.

CROSSING A KING COBRA MALE WITH A BOTTOM SWORD FEMALE
This cross produces all Lace Cobra males and good females for Bottom Sword production.

BREEDING THE KING COBRA IS A TWO GENERATION PLAN. The first generation is shown below. No King Cobras are produced in the first generation. The second generation, when inbred, produce good King Cobras with dark monocles.

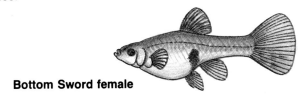

Bottom Sword female

King Cobra male

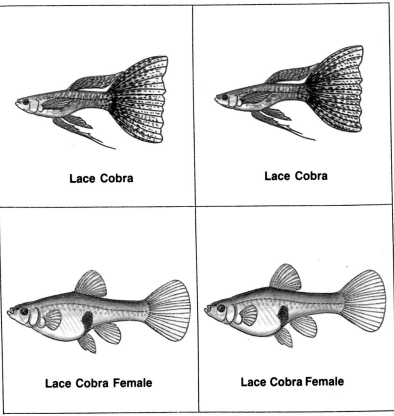

Lace Cobra

Lace Cobra

Lace Cobra Female

Lace Cobra Female

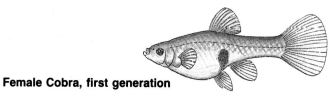

Female Cobra, first generation

King Cobra

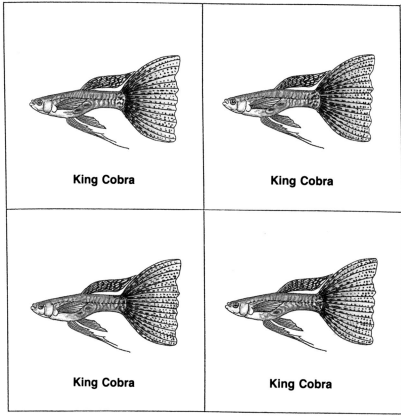

King Cobra

King Cobra

King Cobra

King Cobra

THE SECOND GENERATION, INBRED FROM THE FIRST GENERATION OFFSPRING, WILL PRODUCE 100% KING COBRA MALES.

An F$_1$ produced from crossing an old fashioned Fan Tail male with a Golden Grass female all exhibited metallic green bodies and Leopard fins. Now I intend to cross this F$_1$ with Leopard and make a new type of Leopard.

From the above crossbreeding example you can understand the basic points of selective breeding: the necessity of using seed fish that are at least somewhat established; the fact that actual selective breeding commences with F$_2$; the importance of repeated selection and weeding out over several generations; the aim of producing beautiful and healthy fish.

I have discussed many aspects of guppy selective breeding. By now, you might think guppies are more trouble than they are worth. But spectacular guppies are not something that can be created in a short span of time. The world of guppies is a deep, complex, fascinating world.

RESULTS OF CROSSING A MALE OLD FASHIONED FAN TAIL WITH A FEMALE GOLDEN GRASS. ALL YOUNG HAVE METALLIC GREEN BODIES AND LEOPARD FINS.

Golden Grass

Old Fashioned Fantail

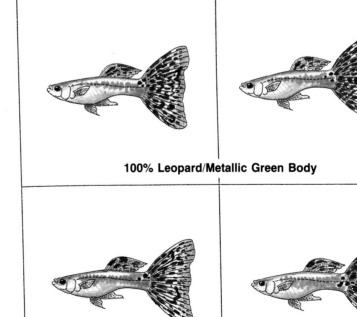

100% Leopard/Metallic Green Body

GUPPY GENETICS

Sex Chromosomes and Sex Limited Genes

Guppies have typical sexually determined genetics, meaning that characteristics such as body color, caudal fin shape, and overall patterning are determined in association with sex (male and female).

The chromosome that determines whether a guppy is male or female is called the sex chromosome. There are two types of sex chromosomes, the X and the Y chromosome. Males inherit a Y chromosome from the father and an X chromosome from the mother, while females have X chromosomes inherited from both the father and the mother. In other words, if the sex chromosomes are XY, the guppy is male; if they're XX, the guppy is female. Colors such as red and blue, caudal fin shapes, patterns, etc., are all carried on the Y chromosome; therefore, these characteristics are only manifested in the male. On the X chromosome there are no equivalent characteristics, so females do not exhibit the sort of coloration or caudal shapes males exhibit. For this reason, shape and color are transmitted from male to male.

Dominance and Recessiveness

In selectively breeding guppies, Mendel's law of dominance is actively applied. Dominance as used in this instance does not mean "superior" ; it means "revealed in the first generation of crossbreeding." Recessiveness refers not to inferiority but to genetic traits that do not appear in the first generation of crossbreeding, remaining dormant.

In other words, traits visible in the F_1 born after mating relatively stable varieties are dominant and hidden characteristics are recessive.

If you cross a King Cobra male with a Grass Tail female, the males in F_1 will all display Cobra traits. We understand from this that the Cobra pattern is dominant. However, in reality it is rare that things go precisely according to the law of dominance in breeding guppies. This is due to the fact that so many of the qualities being transmitted are not completely established. For this reason, characteristics in between those of both parents often show up in F_1.

Incomplete Dominance and Hybrids

If things went exactly according to Mendel's law of dominance, the characteristics of only one parent would be exhibited in F_1, but in breeding guppies such results are rare. More often we see qualities that are midway between those of both parents. The term "incomplete dominance" refers to this imperfect relationship between dominant and recessive traits. The F_1 that displays these qualities of incomplete dominance is called an intermediary hybrid.

Partial Dominance

Within incomplete dominance, the partial traits such as the Cobra pattern appearing in F_1 or the dark blue of the caudal peduncle on the Mosaic are called partial dominance. As partial dominance develops and those qualities become established, a new strain is also established.

The Future of Guppy Genetics

Guppy genetics is not undergoing much academic research in Japan. Even if one tries to investigate genetics formally, it is often problematic because traits are not always manifested as some genetic principles would predict. Furthermore, the existing literature on guppy genetics is largely German and English or American and may not necessarily be applicable to contemporary, Japanese, domestic guppies.

Even if you get an F_2 litter after mating F_1 hybrids, it is not at all useful in studying the overall genetic scheme. The only thing to do is to gradually gather information about dominance and recessiveness through the practical experience of observing your breeding results, using a genetics text for reference.

In breeding any guppy, you always breed a male and female. The female carries the XX sex chromosomes; the male carries the XY chromosomes. You can see that the pair always produce, theoretically, an equal number of males, XY, and females, XX.

	FEMALE XX	
MALE XY	XX	XX
	XY	XY

No. 1 ♀		* ?	†				Origin: *Mair Co.*		Race: *wild*		Treatment: —	

	Mate #	Mated	Separated	Inseminated	Delivery	Hatching	Free Swimming	M-No.	Phenotype of Offspring ♀♀	Phenotype of Offspring ♂♂	Number of Offspring At Delivery	Number of Offspring At Maturity
1	2 ♂	5/23/76	6/1/76		6/14/76			M1I	8 wild + 7 blond	6 wild + 7 blond	30	28
2												
3												
4												
5												
6												
7												
8												
9												
10												

An example of a guppy breeding chart suggested by Dr. J. Schroder in his amazing book GENETICS FOR AQUARISTS. Anyone seriously interested in breeding guppies (or any fish for that matter) should study this book.

ABOVE: Early Painted Tuxedo Guppies. This American strain has disappeared.
LEFT,TOP: Old style Flamingo guppy.
LEFT,BOTTOM: Old style half-black. Photos by Dr. Herbert R. Axelrod.

Suggested Reading

The titles described here, all published by T.F.H. Publications, Inc. and designed to be of special use to guppy enthusiasts, are available at pet shops everywhere.

FISH DISEASES:
A Complete Introduction
By Dr. Gottfried Schubert
Hardcover **CO-016**
ISBN 0-86622-265-0
Softcover **CO-016S**
ISBN 0-86622-297-9
Audience: Anyone keeping an aquarium will sooner or later be faced with a sick fish. Teaching aquarists how to identify, treat and cure fish diseases is the purpose of this book. It is magnificently illustrated with full-color photographs and drawings and has been written by one of the world's leading fish pathologists.
5½ x 8½, 96 pages
Contains over 100 full-color photos.

GUPPY HANDBOOK
By Dr. C. W. Emmens
ISBN 0-87666-084-7
TFH PS-668
Contents: Maintenance. Water Quality. Reproduction of Guppies. Feeding Guppies. Raising the Young. Keeping Guppies Healthy. Guppy Genetics. Selection with Minimal Inbreeding. Reversion to or Towards Type. Color Testing in the Female. Standards for Guppies. Strains of Guppies. Prize-winning Guppies.
Audience: Required reading for all guppy breeders. Text covers areas on measuring and adjusting salinity, saving the young, sex-limited and sex-linked inheritance. Ages 13 and above.
Soft cover, 5½ x 8", 128 pages
31 black and white photos,
63 color photos.

HOW TO RAISE
SHOW GUPPIES
By Lou Wasserman
ISBN 0-87666-453-2
TFH PS-738
Contents: The Gratification of a Guppy Hobbyist. Equipment. Water. Feeding. A Typical Day. Maintaining a Strain. Preparation for Showing. The Show Itself. History of the Modern Day Guppy. Judging Standards.
Audience: This book is intended for fish hobbyists who want to know more about the show circuit on which fancy guppies are entered into show competition and how they can raise guppies of show caliber. High school level.
Highly illustrated in both color and black and white, includes color photos of guppy varieties never before published.
Soft cover, 5½ x 8", 96 pages

GUPPIES—KW-058
By Wilfred L. Whitern
ISBN 0-87666-523-7
Hard cover, contains full-color photos.

LIVEBEARING
AQUARIUM FISHES
By Manfred Brembach
ISBN 0-86622-101-8
T.F.H. PS-832
Contents: What are Livebearers, Keeping Livebearers, Breeding Livebearing Aquarium Fishes, Nutrition, The Mechanics of Livebearing, Behavior of Livebearers, Family Poeciliidae-Typical Livebearers, Family Goodeidae, Family Hemiramphidae-Halfbeaks, Family Jenynsiidae, Family Anablepidae.
Audience: In this useful book author Manfred Brembach takes readers by the hand and leads them through the fascinating hobby of keeping livebearing fish species. He covers every topic of importance from daily care right through breeding the parents and raising the young.
Flexible hardcover, 5½ x 8",
128 pages, 140 full-color photos.

LIVEBEARERS—KW-049
By Wilfred L. Whithern
ISBN 0-87666-518-0
Hard cover, contains full-color photos.

Genetics for the Aquarist
By Dr. J. Schroder
ISBN 0-87666-461-3
TFH PS-656
Written to be of special benefit to beginners, this excellent text explains fish genetics so that breeders can produce better specimens scientifically.
Contents: How to Keep Breeding Records. The Pure Line. Mendel's First and Second Laws. Sex-Linked Inheritance. Interaction of Non-Allelomorphic Genes. Exchange of Genes Between Chromosomes. Founders of Genetics. Mendel's Third Law. Polygenic Inheritance. Polygenic Sex Determination. Melanism and Mottling in the Mollies. Incompatibility of Germ-Cells in the Inheritance of Fin Abnormalities and With Respect to the Color Gene "Fuligonosus." The Action of Suppressor Genes in the Berlin Guppy. Harmful Effects of Genes from Different Species. Inheritance in Modes of Behavior. Variations of Phenotype.
Soft Cover, 5½ x 8", 125 pages
10 black and white photos, 59 color photos, 30 line drawings, 12 tables.

Dr. Axelrod's Mini-Atlas of Freshwater Aquariums
By Dr. Herbert R. Axelrod,
Dr. Warren E. Burgess, Dr. Cliff
W. Emmens, et. al
ISBN 0-86622-385-1
T.F.H. H-1090
The entire staff of TROPICAL FISH HOBBYIST magazine, aided by Prof. C. W. Emmens, pooled their talents to make this the most complete book on aquarium fishes ever published.

This is called the "mini" ATLAS in reference to the much larger DR. AXELROD'S ATLAS, which, in its last edition, had more than 4,000 color photographs of fishes, but which lacked the selection, care, breeding and aquarium plants material. The new ATLAS includes a full-length section treating the most up-to-date methods of aquarium fishes and plant care by one of the world's leading authorities, Dr. Cliff Emmens. The scientific names of the fishes are up-to-date with the most recent, scientifically accepted designations. The text and photos in the new MINI-ATLAS has a separate value to hobbyists: all of the

fishes in the book are cross-referenced by both scientific and common names, making it possible to obtain information about a species even if you don't know its scientific name.

The photographs—over 2200 in full color—provide the same type of exciting eye appeal and identification value that have made the full-size DR. AXELROD'S ATLAS OF FRESHWATER AQUARIUM FISHES such a tremendous winner among fish books and have been carefully selected to include common fishes . . . those that the world's hobbyists would encounter most frequently.

A big FIRST for this book is the pictorial captions, which tell at a glance all the pertinent information the average person needs to know about the fish . . . how it breeds, its temperament, feeding habits, etc. In that way the authors have been able to present a huge amount of information in the smallest possible space.
Hardcover, 5½ x 8½", 992 pages
Over 2200 full-color photos

141

General Index

N

Natural origin, 7, 9-10
"Needle" disease, 98
Neon Tuxedo guppy, 59, 62
—female, 79
Nothobranchius rachovi, 7

O

Oryzias latipes, 7
Outbreeding, 103
Oviparity, 7

P

Pin Tail guppy, 87
Poecilia reticulata, 9
Pregnancy
—marks of, 94

R

Recessiveness, 138
Red Grass guppy, 50
Red Mosaic guppy, 38

Red Tail Cobra guppy, 47
Red Tail Tuxedo guppy, 62
Research group, 11
Reverend John Lechmere
  Guppy, 9
Round Tail guppy, 87

S

Seed fish, 11
—selection of, 92
Selective breeding, 5, 12, 15, 17,
  91
—history of, 33
Sex
—distinguishing, 98
—separating by, 98
Sex chromosomes, 138
Spade Tail guppy, 87
Spawning tank, 94
Sword Tail guppy
— 70 87
—breeding, 111
— female, 80

T

Tail rot, 23

Taxonomical history, 9
Thermostat, 13
Tiger guppy, 70
—breeding, 118
Top Sword guppy
— 70 87
Tubificids, 19
Tuxedo guppy, 59
—breeding, 111

V

Viviparity, 7

W

Water
—adjusting pH of, 16
—changing of, 16-17
—management of, 15-17
Water fleas, 19
Water sprite, 14
Whitespot disease, 22

Y

Yellow Grass guppy, 50

Illustration Index